The Rise of Tech Giants

GLOBAL POLITICS AND SECURITY

Volume 4

Edited by

Prof. Lorenzo Kamel,
University of Turin's History Department,
and Istituto Affari Internazionali (IAI)

PETER LANG

Bern • Berlin • Bruxelles • New York • Oxford

Nicola Bilotta / Simone Romano (eds.)

The Rise of Tech Giants

A Game Changer in Global Finance and Politics

PETER LANG

Bern • Berlin • Bruxelles • New York • Oxford

Bibliographic Information published by the Deutsche Nationalbibliothek
The Deutsche Nationalbibliothek lists this publication in the Deutsche Nationalbibliografie; detailed bibliographic data is available online at http://dnb.d-nb.de.

Library of Congress Cataloging-in-Publication Data
A CIP catalog record for this book has been applied for at the Library of Congress.

This book has been realized thanks to the strategic partnership between IAI and Intesa Sanpaolo and it has been supported by Intesa Sanpaolo.

ISSN 2624-8905
ISBN 978-3-0343-3848-6 (Print) • E-ISBN 978-3-0343-3868-4 (E-PDF)
E-ISBN978-3-0343-3869-1 (EPUB) • E-ISBN 978-3-0343-3870-7 (MOBI)
DOI 10.3726/b15941

This publication has been peer reviewed.

www.peterlang.com

Table of Contents

Figures

Tables

Acknowledgments

This book has come about thanks to the strategic partnership between IAI (Istituto Affari Internazionali) and Intesa Sanpaolo and with the support of Intesa Sanpaolo.

We are especially grateful to all the people and institutions who have contributed and improved this research effort. The list includes Jean-Pierre Darnis, Savino Damico, Hugo Doyle, Laura Grassi, Antonio La Mura, Alessandro Longoni, Mariateresa Maggiolino, Federico Orsi, Francesco Renga, Nicolò Romani, Francesca Rosati, Cristiana Schena, Martina Scopsi, Giancarlo Sfolcini, Alfonso Siano, Mark Smitham, Nadir Snuono, Teresa Spada, Romano Stasi, Alessandra Tanda, Stefania Vigna and Fabrizio Virtuani. And the following institutions: ABI Lab; AssoFintech; Banca d'Italia; Fintech District; the Fintech & Insurtech Observatory of the School of Management-Politecnico di Milano. Intesa Sanpaolo; and Microsoft.

In addition, our thanks go to Franco Passacantando, who has been an invaluable advisor during the entire journey of this project.

This book would have not seen light of day without the support of the staff at IAI who have been involved in this project in different capacities, in particular Alessandra Bertino and Davide Ceccanti.

Last but not least, our deepest gratitude goes to Lorenzo Kamel and the editorial staff of Peter Lang, who have believed in this project.

Franco Passacantando

Foreword

In debates over the impact that FinTech may have on the financial industry, special attention is directed at understanding the implications of the Tech giants' entry into the banking industry. Indeed, after having gained a dominant role in the landscape of internet related activities, companies like Google, Facebook, and Amazon have recently started offering various payments' and consumer finance services.

New competitors to traditional financial intermediaries could in principle be a welcome development, especially by consumers who are eager users of social media and e-services. However, there is some fear that, in the long run, results could be less straightforward, resulting in less rather than more competition. The Tech giants have shown an outstanding capacity to penetrate new markets, given their strength in high tech, the wealth of data they have access to and their very aggressive marketing strategies. After all, the essence of banking is the acquisition, storage and elaboration of information. At a time in which most financial wealth is dematerialized and customers relationships are, to a large extent, no longer based on personal interaction, a key factor of success is the capacity to gain information about consumer preferences, the habits of possible commercial suppliers and even the personal attitudes and opinions of potential clients. A very extensive network of bank branches can even become a competitive disadvantage, given the difficulty of downsizing legacy labor force and physical infrastructure.

Tech giants still play a rather limited role in the financial industry but in other business areas they have reached exponential growth, thanks to their ability to exploit network economies, by which customers start using certain services simply because most other people use them, a very powerful mechanism especially in the payments' industry. There is also growing concern that the acquisition and mismanagement of personal data could eventually constitute a challenge to privacy regulations and even democratic norms. Furthermore, the profit shifting practices of Tech giants who operate in multiple jurisdictions could result in tax base erosion, which would in turn reinforce their dominant position.

One should however be very careful in reaching hasty conclusions about an inevitable decline of the traditional banking industry. The comparative advantages of traditional banks should not be underestimated. The most important one is the trust that customers have in the safety of their bank deposits, and in the payments made in bank money. This trust is the result of a long historical process, which has witnessed repeated refinements of bank regulations and the creation of safety nets, where a key role is played by deposit insurance schemes and central banks' lending of last resort. Furthermore, it is not at all a given that it is in the best interest of Tech giants to compete against banks, which are also some of their most important customers, and to enter into a field with very high costs to comply with existing regulation.

In conclusion it is not clear whether current developments are bound to set in motion a revolutionary change in the financial industry and perhaps in the global political landscape, as some fear, or simply an evolution of existing trends. To shed some light on this complex issue, the International Affairs Institute (IAI), in partnership with Intesa Sanpaolo, has followed an innovative process by putting together a very qualified and diversified group of academic economists, practitioners, and industry representatives who for more than a year have exchanged their views and research on different aspects of the problem.

The result is this book, which I believe is an extremely useful tool for scholars who want to shed light on a very complex and to a large extent unprecedented development. Ultimately it is meant to offer a contribution of analysis and opinions for policy makers who face the difficult task of identifying proper regulation for this industry.

Introduction

In 2017 alone almost 10 million people used Google Pay or Apple Pay to pay for their transactions. In 2016 Amazon financed small enterprises with 1 billion dollars' worth of loans. In that same year Alipay – the financial spin-off of Alibaba – processed 175 million transactions for a total value of $1.7 trillion. Tech giants entering the banking and financial industry is not an issue of the future: it is already happening. This phenomenon has crucial implications that extend well beyond the banking system. The key questions are indeed manifold: will tech giants be competitors of incumbents in the near future, or will they partner up? How will financial regulation handle this radical change and will it succeed in creating a level playing field? What are the implications from a political and social point of view? Will tech giants acquire too much bargaining power in dealing with sovereign states, allowing them to steer laws and political decision in their favour?

The Istituto Affari Internazionali (IAI), in partnership with Intesa Sanpaolo, has carried out a research project aimed at studying the economic and political implications of tech giants entering the banking industry. The results of this analysis – carried out with the active participation of many institutions and experts – are presented in this book, which has two parts. The first comprises five chapters. The first chapter discusses the main barriers and comparative advantages faced by the tech giants in penetrating the banking industry, focusing particularly on the issues of trust and reputation and the ability to add value by exploiting big data and technology innovations. The second chapter illustrates – through practical examples – the different business models that tech giants are bringing into the financial sector, which are bound to reshape the way incumbents do business, at least in certain sectors of the banking supply chain. The third chapter looks at the key issue of regulation, discussing the way regulators are handling this (r)evolution and the implications of the new regulatory frameworks, such as PSD2 in Europe and Open Banking in the UK. The fourth chapter takes a close look at the case studies of Alibaba in China and Rakuten in Japan. The Asian economic, financial and social context is fundamentally different to the Western one but studying these two examples of tech champions that have set up their own financial institution offers many useful insights into a reality which is rapidly changing in the West also. The fifth chapter addresses many still unanswered questions about the key political and policy implications that stem from this radical innovation. It shows how the penetration of tech giants in the banking sector creates issue that go well beyond the mere economic sphere, presenting challenges of a political, fiscal and social nature, at national and international level.

The second part of the book presents six focuses, authored by experts, academics, practitioners and representatives of both banks and Fintech (financial technology) organizations. They have participated actively in the research effort throughout its development and their contributions are intended to shed light on key specific issues that characterize the topics analysed in the first part. The first work, authored by Filippo Renga, Laura Grassi and Nadir Snouno, presents an overview of the Italian Fintech ecosystem and its present development. The second, written by the Italian Banking Association (ABI), explains the key challenges that incumbents have to face but also the tools that they possess to defend their position, such as their historic competence in financial services and their trust relationship with clients. The third piece of work, whose authors are Cristiana Schena and Alessandra Tanda, looks deeper into the business models being brought by the Big Tech companies into the banking industry. The fourth, by Mariateresa Maggiolino, concentrates on the antitrust perspective, highlighting how the entrance of these giants, although they share a dominant position in many markets, could result in a wider variety of products with a lower cost, and possibly end up enhancing the functioning of the market, profiting consumers. The fifth, written by Fabrizio Virtuani, describes in detail the role of the main technology innovations in shaping this revolution, in banking and beyond. The sixth and final focus, by Nicolò Romani and Giancarlo Sfolcini, analyses deeply the issue of digital identity protection, closely connected to the Techfin revolution.

The progressive penetration of tech giants into the banking and financial services industry has, at least potentially, a radical impact. It has already been changing the structure and relative powers in the market, affecting deeply the business models, urging regulators to develop new frameworks and posing challenges to fiscal systems and democratic architecture. Albeit complicated, variegated and with possible side-effects, the dynamics analysed in this book bring not only risks, but also innovations and opportunities. The key challenge facing all the actors is maximizing the positive impacts while minimizing the threats. Will we – as society, business community and political leadership – be up to the challenge?

Part One

Nicola Bilotta and Simone Romano

Chapter 1: Comparative Advantages

1.1 Technology: a crucial component

Technological innovations and digitalization are transforming the banking industry at an unprecedented rate. In what can be described as the fourth industrial revolution (Schwab 2016), Fintech (financial technology) has radically affected each segment of the banking supply chain. According to the Bank of International Settlements (BIS), the term Fintech covers digital innovations and technology-enabled business model innovations in the financial sector (Phillipon 2017: 6). More specifically, this neologism may refer to start-ups, incumbents and Internet firms which make use of technological innovations and the digitalization of financial services to develop innovative products in the most profitable segments of the banking industry (Caretto et al. 2018).

After an initial sunk cost investment, the exploitation of technology and data allows overall transaction costs to be reduced, resulting in new business opportunities for both incumbents and new entrants. Three segments within the banking industry are primarily impacted by Fintech innovations: payments; personal finance; and lending (Efma 2016: 8).

As shown by a 2016 McKinsey report, new digital players are already eroding margins from incumbents: the profits of traditional financial institutions are concentrated in the origination[1] and sales side of banking, which account for 65 per cent of the industry profits and cover activities such as insurance, asset management, retail and wholesale payment transactions (including remittances and international payments) (McKinsey 2016). According to another McKinsey report published in 2017, many of these activities (like payments, consumer finance and asset management) are the segments in which incumbents will experience the largest fee and margin reduction due to digitalization (Dietz et al. 2017).

---

1 Origination is the multi-step process every individual must go through when obtaining a mortgage or home loan, as well as other types of personal loan. During this process, borrowers must submit various types of financial information and documentation to a mortgage lender, including tax return payment history, credit card information and bank balances. Mortgage lenders use this information to determine the type of loan and the interest rate for which the borrower is eligible.

The digitalization of the banking supply chain has affected consumer habits as well, shifting from human interaction through branches to multi-channel interaction through online and mobile apps (Figure 1).

Figure 1: New ways of banking.

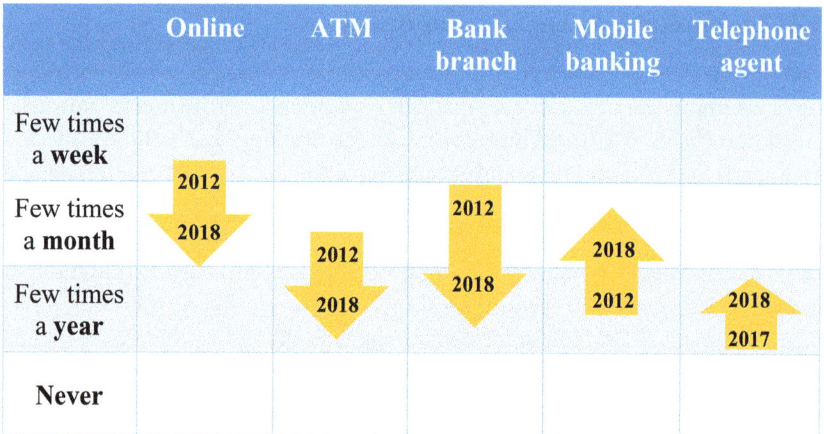

Source: Authors' elaboration from PwC (2018).

In this evolving financial landscape, incumbents are experiencing fiercer vertical and horizontal competition. New digital entrants may be threatening banks' customer relationships and eroding fees from the retail and commercial segments.

These dynamics follow three major trends. First, the digitalization of products and services has increased the disintermediation between banks and clients (Schena et al. 2018): since consumers interact with third-providers using the Web, banks are losing direct contact with their clients. Second, consumers benefit from online comparative tools, reducing the information asymmetry of consumers and gaining the possibility of choosing different providers for different needs. Third, since the 2008 financial crisis consumers have partially reduced their trust in banks, which are still struggling to rebuild it.

Fintech start-ups are not the only ones penetrating the banking sector. The possibility of monetizing the huge of amount data gathered carrying out their primary business has paved the way for large technological and non-financial companies (Dietz et al. 2017) (such as Alibaba and Amazon) to stake a claim on banks' customers, revenues and profits (Blomstrom 2018). Some believe this move into financial services is simply a natural extension of the current offer of tech giants commonly known as GAFA (which stands for Google, Apple, Facebook and

Amazon) (Meirion-Williams 2017). In fact, it could be part of a broader strategy, allowing these players to expand the range of their offering in order to become even more relevant in consumers' lives (Accenture 2016: 3).

In analysing the possible entrance of GAFA-like companies into the banking and financial industry, it is important to clarify the difference between Fintech and Techfin. According to Jack Ma, founder of the Alibaba group, the term Techfin defines technological non-financial companies that are entering the financial market but, while Fintech improves the technology of the existing financial system, 'Techfin is to rebuild the system with technology' (Zen 2016). This implies that Techfin companies start with technology and wonder how to use it to change finance, while Fintech starts with finance and uses technology to improve it and make it more profitable (Skinner 2018).

Techfin companies, starting with technology and data, begin their relationship with customers in a non-financial service setting. This allows them to collect massive amounts of data from those relationships and then seek to make use of the collected data in the banking market. This can usually take two forms: one indirect, where Techfin companies sell their data to financial services providers or serve as a conduit through which their customers can access financial services provided by a separate institution; a second one direct, with Techfin companies providing financial services directly themselves (Zetzsche et al. 2017: 9).

Since Techfin companies are like ecosystems, banking services can be integrated into their value chain: while shopping on an Amazon e-commerce platform, customers can use Amazon Pay to make faster payments; similarly, anyone can make online purchases using Google Wallet or send money to a friend through Facebook Pay.

The Techfin trend is already a structured reality in Asia, where non-financial companies like Alibaba and Rakuten have taken full advantage of softer regulatory systems and less developed banking markets to enter the industry. Albeit less structured, giant technology companies have started offering different forms of financial services in Western economies as well. According to a 2018 PwC survey, 83 per cent of the respondent senior bankers thought that Google and Amazon would be mainstream banking providers in the next ten years (Panebianco 2018: 6).

Figure 2: Top 10 retail-banking trends and predictions for 2018.

Source: Authors' elaboration from Marous (2017).

Established technological giants or brand-new Fintech start-ups, due to their own technological and non-financial nature, can face both advantages and disadvantages when it comes to entering the banking sector and competing with the existing players. The paragraphs that follow look deeper into some of them.

1.2 Reputation and trust

In business, as famously pointed out by Warren Buffett, a good reputation is hard to earn and easy to lose (Beman 2014). It is built, like trust, on the continuous interaction between a company's service or product and a client's satisfaction. The more a customer learns to trust an agent, the more comfortable they will feel with relying on that agent in the long term. Trust is therefore based on the experience that an agent has fulfilled our expectations in the past, creating confidence that that same agent will fulfil our expectations in the future as well, cementing existing relations and attracting new ones (Eisenegger 2009). Despite computerization and regulation having mitigated the need for personal trust, reputation still plays a key role in incentivizing or disincentivizing a commercial relationship.

It follows that trust and reputation still have a direct business impact, especially on banking (Buckley and Nixon 2009). The relationship between banks and their consumers is positively related to perceived security, privacy, usability, reputation, trust and commitment, especially when it comes to online banking in which perceived risks and uncertainty are higher. The lack of a solid reputation in this context could be a serious constraint for new entrants, which need to gain the trust of potential customers first, unlike incumbents that can count on consolidated relationships. However, since the financial crisis, banks are experiencing a lowering of their reputation (Vanston 2009). According to the 2018

Edelman Trust Barometer,[2] the financial services industry was trusted the least by consumers, with half of the banks' customers saying they did not trust them, albeit figures having slightly improved (rising from 48 per cent in 2014 to 54 per cent in 2018). In contrast, the technology industry is the most trusted – with an approval rating of around 75 per cent.

The comparison can certainly be misleading: for a consumer, trusting a particular brand of phone does not involve needing to feel the same level of security as when trusting the company managing their money. Nonetheless, the very positive reputation and the strong relationship of trust that GAFA companies have managed to build with their customers could play a decisive role if they were to enter the banking industry.

Figure 3: Would you trust them with your money?

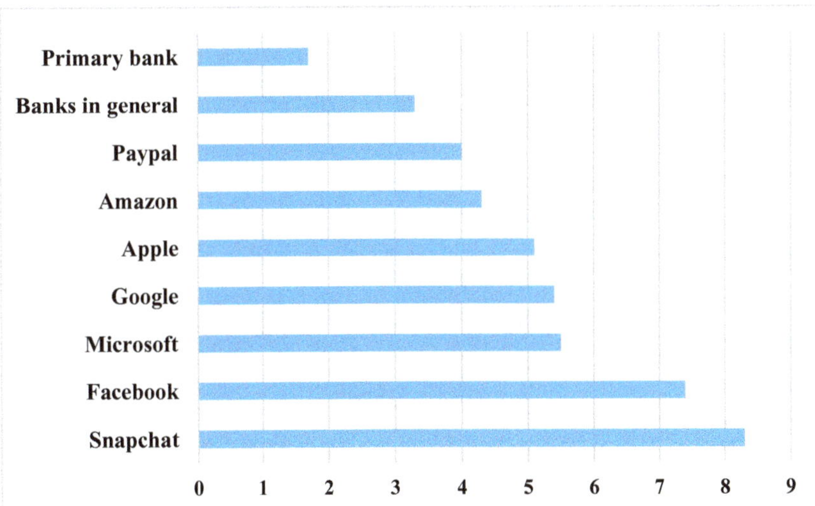

Source: Authors' elaboration from du Toit and Cheris (2018).

As shown by a 2016 Ernst & Young's report, customers who bank with non-traditional players trust them as much as they do the incumbent players, or even more so (Ernst & Young 2016: 5–6). Among new providers, established giants like Amazon

2 The Edelman Trust Barometer is an annual survey which measures trust among consumers in different countries. See Edelman (2018).

have been able to establish a brand considered to be reliable well beyond the boundaries of their traditional business. A survey carried out by Bain & Co. in 2018 (du Toit and Cheris 2018) shows a similar picture, with an average of more than 50 per cent of respondents open to buying financial products from tech companies, a trend likely to increase over time since younger respondents were the most willing to do so.[3] Furthermore, American and British consumers rank Amazon and Paypal almost as high as banks for trust with their money (du Toit and Cheris 2018) (Figure 3).

Despite the negative repercussions of the financial crisis, traditional banks seem to continue to enjoy a comparative advantage in terms of established relations and trust. Nonetheless, the increasing interest of consumers in Techfin companies as providers of banking services and products is undeniable. A study carried out by Financial Brand breaking down Google Search Trends confirms this, showing how Facebook Bank and Google Bank were highly searched (Figure 4).

Figure 4: Desire for GAFA banks.

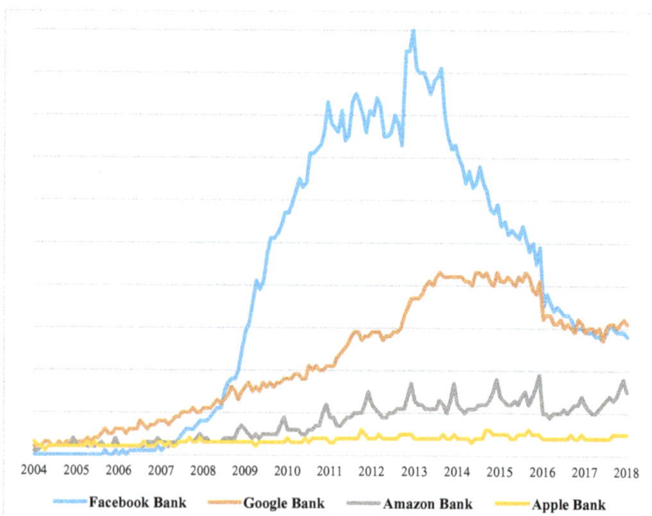

Source: Authors' elaboration from Google Trends.

3 These trends are also confirmed by an Accenture report (2016). Consumers are potentially interested in banking services and products offered by Techfins. Younger consumers are attracted to these opportunities the most. According to the report, 40 per cent, 37 per cent and 34 per cent of people aged 18 to 34 years old declared to be open to banking services offered by Google, Amazon and Apple respectively. The percentages significantly decrease when older generations are taken into account.

To better understand this pattern, it is important to look at Techfin business models. Apple, Amazon, Google and Facebook[4] are among the world's best 'belonging' brands (IBM Ix 2017): as their products and services have become an indispensable part of the consumer's daily life, these companies have been able to create a collective imagination behind their brands (Vivaldi 2018), developing interactions with consumers on everyday enrichment, compelling relationships and emphatic innovation. Moreover, the development of the Internet of Things economy is blurring the traditional barriers between sectors, producing a landscape in which consumers ask for similar experiences regardless of the kind of industry (Moneta 2014: 3).

It is important to add that Techfins' business strategy is not product-driven but customer-centric, having each current and prospective customer at the centre of the business and operating models (Moneta 2014: 12). This becomes of a strategic importance considering that banks' clients have increased their demand for a better customer experience and easier access to services and products.

The customer-centric business models of Techfins have allowed them to gain a solid reputation and make consumers feel as if they belong to an ecosystem of services and products tailored to them. This is the key reason why consumers might purchase banking products and services offered by Techfins rather than by established banks, despite the incumbents being more established in the field (and should therefore, in theory, be considered more trustworthy). Yet consumers could trust non-financial companies for specific banking activities, such as payments, but not for riskier or more complicated activities.

1.3 Information accumulation and big data analysis

In the current economy, data is like gold or, even better, the new oil: pushing companies to find, extract, refine and monetize data (Barberis 2016). Also, in banking, the applications for data are countless.

For many years, incumbents have enjoyed a great advantage due to the accumulation of financial information on their clients. In fact, banks have traditionally been the providers with the most extensive datasets on savers' behaviours and financial history.

Nowadays, the interaction between data and technology is changing the financial industry across three dimensions: data storage and processing; data transfer; and data availability (Bofondi and Gobbi 2017: 109). The digitalization of the

---

4 In the top 25 belonging brands, Apple ranked first, Amazon second, Google seventh and Facebook twenty-second.

current economy has produced a huge amount of valuable information, the so-called big data. Big data can easily and cheaply be transferred through the Internet without dedicated networks, while cloud computing allows them to be stored and processed.

Having access to big data (and possessing the know-how to exploit them) has become a key driver of growth. Banks can more accurately evaluate credit risk assessment, for instance. Predictive analytics exploit big data to simultaneously analyse credit history, loan applications and extra information such as social media feedback. For example American Express has developed predictive models to analyse historical transactions and 115 variables to forecast customer churn. The profile of a potential borrower is thus deeply scanned through variables which were previously unavailable. Similarly, big data improve the effectiveness of anti-money-laundering efforts.

In addition, big data enhances personalized communication and real-time solutions through behavioural marketing. Banks can therefore offer financial and insurance products tailored *ad hoc* for individual clients. Singapore Citibank, for example, offers customer discounts at retailers and restaurants based on customer transactional patterns (Porras 2018).

Big data, then, enhance banks' productivity, improve their risk control and increase profitability (Garg et al. 2017). However, the key is not only having access to a huge amount of data, but also possessing the capabilities to exploit them properly, finding useful information in a sea of data.

Quoting Francisco Gonzàlez (2014),

> 'Banks hold huge stores of information about their customers, and this is a crucial competitive edge. If banks can convert that information into knowledge, they can use it to offer customers goods and services that better meet their needs. But to do this, banks will need to develop a completely different platform concept from scratch – one that is able to integrate vast quantities of customer data seamlessly and without interruption.'

In order to extract value from data, banks need firstly to develop the infrastructure to store and process information from all the available sources. Secondly, they need to obtain the know-how and the technological capabilities to work with the data collected. Finally, banks need to assess how they can exploit their data in order to maximize new models and opportunities for their businesses. Banks are fully aware of the potential of data exploitation and of what is needed to make the most of this; in fact, in 2016 alone the banking sector invested around $13 billion in IT analytics.

Big data analytics unlock opportunities to improve banking efficiency but at the same time they are making the banking sector more competitive. Techfins developed their core business exploiting digital and technological innovations, being data driven since day zero (Barberis 2016). Therefore, Techfins have already developed the infrastructures, the technological capabilities and the in-house human capital to work with big data. While Techfins are digital, banks need to go digital. It is no surprise then that Techfins' data accumulation is better than the data sets of traditional banks, for several reasons. First, Techfins' data collection is obtained from various sources that combined provide a comprehensive databased view of their customers' preferences and behaviours (Zetzsche et al. 2017: 10). Second, Techfins can extract data from a much larger section of the population than traditional banks: while the latter only have access to their clients' information, the former leverage data from all consumers that interact with their core business activities. Facebook records more than 2 billion users and Apple sold last year more than 227 million products,[5] while HSBC, Europe's largest bank, recorded 38 million clients in 2018. Third, incumbents can only get data from the back-end of a business transaction, which may provide information on cash flow processed in a bank account and on a client's income and expense statement. Techfins, meanwhile, enjoy a front-end relationship in a business transaction, enabling Techfin companies to form a more accurate picture than any bank can of the real financial position of the business to which they are considering extending credit or insurance or other financial services. Techfin companies will know whether a certain amount of cash represents a loan from another source or income from customers' sales and they will also know whether the retailer or manufacturer enjoys low or high rates of product returns and will be able to infer to some extent whether its customers are happy and satisfied (Zetzsche et al. 2017: 16–7).

Google provides the perfect example: it gathers information on its accounts combining data from its different services and products. It stores all the activity of its customers during their use of the Google online search engine. Through Google Maps, Google knows where a person has been, keeping track of how much time a person has spent in any location – such as a bar, a shop, and so on. Google also stores information on which apps are installed on their clients' devices and has access to all consumers' history on YouTube. Exploiting the accumulation of information from all these different sources, Google creates an individual advertisement profile to target specific sales in relation to consumer behaviours.

---

5 See Statista website: *Most famous social network sites worldwide as of January 2019, ranked by number of active users (in millions)*, https://www.statista.com/statistics/272014; and *Global Apple iPhone sales from 3rd quarter 2007 to 4th quarter 2018 (in million units)*, https://www.statista.com/statistics/263401.

Nevertheless, it is important to point out that having access to a consumer's profile, however detailed, may produce a distorted image of their financial condition. This means that while their accumulation of information may provide them with a clear picture of what a consumer desires or what they have bought online, if Techfin companies cannot access a consumer's bank account, they will not know their real financial situation. Banks, meanwhile, have historical information that allows them to assess the true financial situation of their clients, although they are missing better understanding of consumer preferences. Banks and Techfins have therefore access to different kinds of information, which provide them with a divergent picture of a person's profile.

Furthermore, the issue of veracity needs to be raised. When consumers go online, they can decide to not to provide their real data or to share just partial personal information. On the contrary, banks implement identity management systems that create legally recognized profiles (Accenture 2013). Giant tech companies have realized the economic value of having access to reliable identities and they have begun working on linking online and offline identities (Krotoski 2012), but they are far from having a secure identification system such as the one put in place by banks.

A further point that is worth considering is the increasing awareness of consumers about the value of their personal data. Voluntary data sharing by consumers is generally connected to subsequent rewards or promotional offers. When a consumer uses the Google search engine, they are using a free tool which helps them find their way online. When somebody creates a Facebook profile, they use a free social network. In exchange for free services and products, these platforms collect and monetize the personal data of consumers using their services.

Until recently, the majority of consumers were unaware of the value of the personal information they were indirectly offering to these platforms. Nowadays, though, according to a survey carried out by Deloitte in 2017 (Pingitore et al. 2017), consumers are more willing to share personal data when they feel they are getting a reward or benefit – the so-called return on data. Moreover, they are more concerned about data privacy. How this increased awareness about the importance of personal data is going to affect GAFA brands, platforms, services and products is still not clear, but it seems very likely that, in the near future, they will keep their comparative advantages by making the most of big data to enhance their businesses.

References

Accenture (2013), *The Future of Identity in Banking*, https://www.accenture.com/_acnmedia/Accenture/Conversion-Assets/DotCom/Documents/Global/PDF/Dualpub_9/Accenture-Future-Identity-Banking.pdf.

Accenture (2016), *Beyond the Everyday Bank*, https://www.accenture.com/_acnmedia/PDF-10/Accenture-Banking-Beyond-Everyday-Bank-pdf.pdf.

Barberis, Janos (2016), 'From Fintech to Techfin: Data Is the New Oil', in *The Asian Banker*, 16 May, http://www.theasianbanker.com/updates-and-articles/from-fintech-to-techfin:-data-is-the-new-oil.

Beman, James (2014), 'The Three Essential Warren Buffett Quotes to Live By', in *Forbes*, 20 April, https://www.forbes.com/sites/jamesberman/2014/04/20/the-three-essential-warren-buffett-quotes-to-live-by.

Blomstrom, Duena (2018), *Emotional Banking. Fixing Culture, Leveraging Fintech, and Transforming Retail Banks into Brands*, Cham, Palgrave Macmillan.

Bofondi, Marcello and Giorgio Gobbi (2017), 'The Big Promise of Fintech', in *European Economy. Banks, Regulation, and the Real Sector*, No. 2017.2 (December), p. 107–119, https://european-economy.eu/book/fintech-and-banks-friends-or-foes.

Buckley, Ross P. and Justen Nixon (2009), 'The Role of Reputation in Banking', in *The Journal of Banking and Finance Law and Practice*, Vol. 20, No. 1 (March), p. 37–50.

Caretto, Giusi et al., eds (2018), *Libro bianco su Fintech e pagamenti digitali*, Roma, Innovative Publishing, https://www.startmag.it/wp-content/uploads/Fintech_Web-260218.pdf.

Dietz, Miklòs et al. (2017), 'Remaking the Bank for an Ecosystem World', in *McKinsey Articles*, October, http://bit.ly/2yPxI4h.

du Toit, Gerard and Aaron Cheris (2018), "Banking's Amazon Moment", in *Bain & Co. Briefs*, 5 March, https://www.bain.com/insights/bankings-amazon-moment.

Edelman Group (2018), *2018 Edelman Trust Barometer Global Report*, January, https://www.edelman.com/research/2018-edelman-trust-barometer.

Efma (2016), *Digital Transformation. The Challenges and Opportunities Facing Banks*, February, http://www.oracle.com/us/industries/financial-services/efma-digital-transformation-wp-2904165.pdf.

Eisenegger, Mark (2009), 'Trust and Reputation in the Age of Globalisation', in Joachim Klewes and Robert Wreschniok, eds, *Reputation Capital. Building and Maintaining Trust in the 21st Century*, Berlin, Springer, p. 11–22.

Ernst&Young (2016), *Trust: Without It, You're Just Another Bank. EY's 2016 Global Consumer Banking Survey*, https://www.ey.com/gl/en/industries/financial-services/banking---capital-markets/ey-trust-without-it-youre-just-another-bank.

Garg, Amit et al. (2017), 'Analytics in Banking: Time to Realize Value', in *McKinsey Articles*, April, http://bit.ly/2hAyuLO.

Gonzàlez, Francisco (2014), 'Knowledge Banking for a Hyperconnected Society', in *MIT Technology Review*, 3 March, https://www.technologyreview.com/s/525106.

IBM Ix (2017), *Brand Belonging: Human Need. Business Opportunity.*

Koechlein, Frank (2016), 'Maximizing Marketing ROI with Data Analytics', in *The Financial Brand*, 9 December, https://thefinancialbrand.com/62466.

Krotoski, Aleks (2012), 'Online Identity: Is Authenticity or Anonymity More Important?', in *The Guardian*, 19 April, https://gu.com/p/37xcm.

Marous, Jim (2017), 'Top 10 Retail Banking Trends and Predictions for 2018', in *The Financial Brand*, 22 December, https://thefinancialbrand.com/69180.

McKinsey (2016), *A Brave New World for Global Banking: McKinsey Global Banking Annual Review 2016*, December, http://bit.ly/2ySiziW.

Meirion-Williams, Richard (2017), 'How Can Banks Counteract the GAFA Threat?', in *Finance Monthly*, 17 October, https://www.finance-monthly.com/?p=16276.

Moneta, Andrea (2014), 'The Customer-centric Insurer in the Digital Era', in *The Digital Insurer*, August, https://www.accenture.com/t20150523T033833__w__/sg-en/_acnmedia/Accenture/Conversion-Assets/DotCom/Documents/Global/PDF/Dualpub_9/Accenture-The-Customer-Centric-Insurer-In-The-Digital-Era.pdf.

Panebianco, Mauro (2018), *Il possibile impatto in economia e finanza dei GAFA*, Pwc Presentation, 14 June, https://www.pwc.com/it/it/industries/asset-management/assets/docs/impatto-economico-finanziario-gafa.pdf.

Phillipon, Thomas, ed. (2017), 'The Fintech Opportunity', in *BIS Working Papers*, No. 655 (August), https://www.bis.org/publ/work655.htm.

Pingitore, Gina et al. (2017), 'To Share or Not to Share. What Consumers Really Think About Sharing Their Personal Information', in *Deloitte Insights*, 5 September, https://www2.deloitte.com/insights/us/en/industry/retail-distribution/sharing-personal-information-consumer-privacy-concerns.html.

Porras, Castaño, Javier (2018), 'Data Analytics, Artificial Intelligence and Big Data in Banking', in *OpenMind*, 16 April, https://www.bbvaopenmind.com/en/economy/finance/data-analytics-artificial-intelligence-and-big-data-in-banking.

PwC (2018), *2018 Digital Banking Consumer Survey: Mobile Users Set the Agenda*, June, https://www.pwc.com/us/en/industries/financial-services/library/digital-banking-consumer-survey.html.

Schena, Cristiana et al. (2018), 'Lo sviluppo del Fintech. Opportunità e rischi per l'industria finanziaria nell'era digitale', in *Quaderni FinTech*, No. 1 (March), http://www.consob.it/web/area-pubblica/ft1.

Schwab, Klaus (2016), *The Fourth Industrial Revolution*, Cologny/Geneva, World Economic Forum.

Skinner, Chris (2018), 'The Difference between FinTech and TechFin', in *The Finanser*, June, https://wp.me/p77S7f-71B.

Vanston, Nick (2009), 'Trust and Reputation in Financial Services', in *Driver Review*, No. 30, https://www.bl.uk/collection-items/trust-and-reputation-in-financial-services.

Vivaldi (2018), 'Brand Strategy: How GAFA Gains Their Ground', in *Vivaldi Blog*, 29 January, http://vivaldigroup.com/en/blogs/leadership-lessons-gafa.

Zen, Soo (2016), 'Techfin: Jack Ma Coins Term to Set Alipay's Goal to Give Emerging Markets Access to Capital', in *South China Morning Post*, 2 December, https://www.scmp.com/tech/article/2051249/techfin-jack-ma-coins-term-set-alipays-goal-give-emerging-markets-access.

Zetzsche, Dirk et al. (2017), 'From FinTech to TechFin: The Regulatory Challenges of Data-Driven Finance', in *EBI Working Paper Series*, No. 6 (April), https://dx.doi.org/10.2139/ssrn.2959925.

Nicola Bilotta and Simone Romano

Chapter 2: Business Models and Strategies

So far, tech giants have entered the banking market at different speeds and to various extents, but payment activities seem to be the most attractive segment of the banking supply chain for Techfin. This is due mainly to the nature of their core businesses, grounded on generating valuable customer data.

Table 1: GAFA and financial services.

	Google	**Apple**	**Facebook**	**Amazon**
Mobile payments	Google Pay	Apple Pay	n/a	Amazon Pay Places
Online payments	Google Pay	Apple Pay	n/a	Amazon Pay
Peer2peer payments	Google Wallet	Apple Pay Cash	Payment in Messenger	n/a
Other payments	n/a	n/a	n/a	Amazon Cash
Lending to customers	Google Store Financing	n/a	n/a	Amazon Lending
Lending to business	n/a	n/a	n/a	Amazon Lending
eMoney	n/a	n/a	n/a	Amazon Coins
App stores	Google Pay	App Store	n/a	Amazon Apps
Voice banking interfaces	Google Home	Siri	n/a	Amazon Alexa

Source: Authors' elaboration from Panebianco (2018).

The global payment landscape has indeed already experienced systemic changes due to technological and digital innovations. This transformation is likely to continue, transforming the industry and increasing competition (Khan et al. 2016). By way of example, despite debit and credit cards remaining the most-used means of e-commerce payments, the number of transactions carried out by e-wallets is rapidly increasing, as Figure 5 shows.

Figure 5: E-commerce payments in 2016.

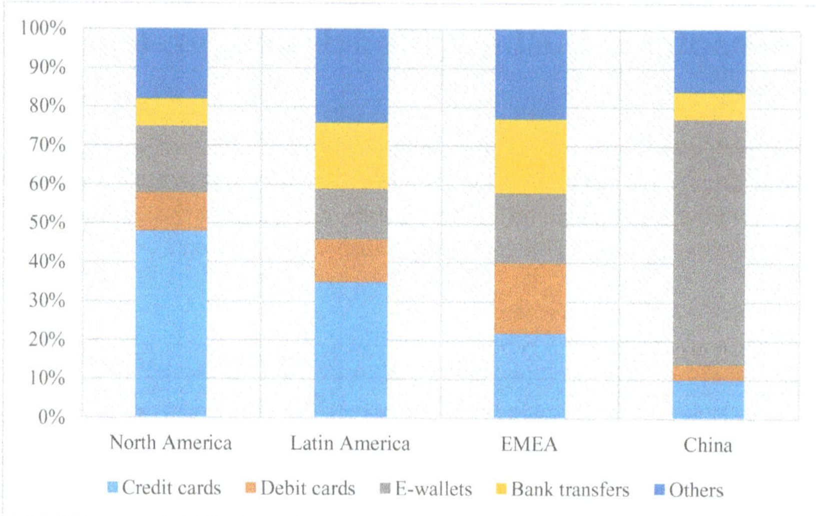

Source: Authors' elaboration from S&P (2018).

According to Standard & Poor's, in 2016 China stood out with 60 per cent of transactions carried out through e-wallets while in the EMEA (Europe, the Middle East and Africa) region, e-wallets were only marginal means of payment, accounting for just 15 per cent of transactions (S&P 2018). China is the leading market in mobile payments, with a total valuation of around $43 trillion in 2017 (Research and Markets 2018). However, according to Forrester (2017), in seven EU countries mobile payments will triple by 2021, increasing from 52 billion euro in 2015 to 148 billion euro, creating the opportunity for a subsequent growth in e-wallets.

In order to give a more detailed view of the strategies used by tech giants in their entry into the banking and financial sector, and to better characterize the business models they have adopted, the following two paragraphs will focus on some practical examples.

2.1 Amazon

Among tech giants, Amazon seems to be the most active so far, in providing financial services that rely on the interaction between the Amazon e-commerce platform, merchants and customers.

Not surprisingly, Amazon has been particularly dynamic in the payment industry, considering that reducing friction for customers by making payment easier is key to boosting Amazon's core business. By 2009, Amazon had developed Amazon Web Pay, a free online money transfer service that allowed users to send digital cash to anyone by email, using a credit card or an Amazon account. This peer-to-peer payment service was shut down in 2014 (Protalinski 2014) but in 2013 Amazon introduced the 'Pay and log in with Amazon' service which enabled customers to use their Amazon credentials to pay third-party merchants (Panzarino 2013).

Furthermore, Amazon Pay is a payment network and a digital wallet for online and bricks-and-mortar consumers and merchants. It manages transactions between buyers and sellers, and simplifies customer check-out processes and merchants' access to buyers' credit card information. Independent shops can link up with Amazon Pay so clients can use their stored credit card information in other shops without setting up new payment accounts.[1] When using Amazon Pay, merchants agree to pay for the service a fixed authorization fee of $0.30 and an additional processing fee (2.9 per cent domestic and 3.9 per cent cross-border),[2] which are divided between Amazon, card issuers and payment networks (Surane and Soper 2018).

Amazon is also working on a payment tool with disruptive potential: Amazon Go, a biometrics payment technology which allows clients to walk out of an offline retail shop without physically checking out to pay. With the implementation of an integrated system of computer vision, sensor fusion and machine learning, linked with Amazon App, shoppers can simply grab their products and go, reducing payment friction and avoiding queues. So far, Amazon has opened seven shops in the US equipped with Amazon Go technology.[3] As observed by Lin Grosman, the Amazon Effect – encouraging offline retailers to offer a consumer experience similar to that of online stores – is likely to boost grab-and-go services in offline retailers and improve their competitiveness (Grosman 2018). If this were the case and Amazon were to provide the needed IT infrastructure, this would allow the tech giants to capture substantially more information on consumer habits outside Amazon.com.

In 2014, Amazon also launched Amazon Coins to further integrate its payment services offering. Amazon Coins is an e-money that allows customers to buy apps, games and digital in-app items at discounted prices (Freedman 2016),

---

1 In 2016, Amazon Pay was used by around 33 million customers worldwide (Perez 2017).

2 See Amazon Pay website: *Merchants*, https://pay.amazon.com/us/merchant.

3 To shop in an Amazon Go, customers need to have an Amazon account and the app Amazon Go installed on their smartphone.

making the purchase of apps easier for customers and attracting more developers to Amazon Marketplace.

Lastly, in 2017 Amazon Cash was introduced in the US to incentivize online selling and to attract consumers without credit or debit cards. Consumers can deposit cash on their digital Amazon accounts at bricks-and-mortar retail partners – such as 7–11 stores – and use the deposited money to make purchases on Amazon.com. A related activity is Amazon Allowance – introduced in 2015 and which is now included in Amazon Cash – that allows parents to set up an Amazon account for their children, who can use the funds in their Amazon Allowance to purchase on Amazon.com.

Beyond payment services, in 2011 Amazon launched in Japan, the UK and the US a lending service to micro, small and medium businesses who operate on its e-commerce platform. Up to 2016, Amazon Lending funded 20,000 merchants, issuing loans for $3 billion, of which $1 billion in 2016 alone (Arora 2017). In 2017, Reuters wrote that Amazon Lending will soon expand in Canada, France, India and China (Dastin 2017). The success of Amazon Lending is grounded on the reduced information asymmetry between the platform and its sellers, as Amazon analyses their selling history to determine how a merchant is likely to perform in the coming months. As these types of merchant mainly rely on Amazon e-commerce marketplace revenues, Amazon can also enforce an efficient counter-moral hazard strategy, freezing the merchants' accounts in the case that they do not repay their loans. Amazon Lending's business plan is to 'enmesh customers and merchants in the company's web, reinforcing one another and strengthening Amazon's grip' (McLannahan 2017). It follows that Amazon Lending benefits Amazon for two main reasons: first, it allows Amazon to earn interest on loans; and second, it generates extra commissions when these merchants increase their sales.

Amazon has also been active in the credit card market, offering the Amazon Prime Store Card and Prime Rewards Visa Signature Card. In Mexico, Amazon has launched a debit card –Amazon Rechargeable – which allows customers to easily load it in convenience stores and to make purchases on the Amazon platform and other online shops such as Netflix, Uber and Spotify (Solomon 2018). In India, Amazon has gone a step further, having delivery staff who take cash deposits at customers' doors. Customers can then pay for their deliveries in cash, and they can deposit additional money for future purchases. The Cashload service also allows customers to pay bills through partner websites and apps and to deposit from credit cards and banking accounts up to 10,000 rupees ($143 – a significant amount of money considering that Indian average income is $50) (Cocheo 2018).

All the tools described improve the efficiency of Amazon's ecosystem and encourage its customers to interact more with its platform, enabling them to access various banking services within Amazon.

2.2 Google, Apple and Facebook

Apple and Google have both developed mobile payment apps built to integrate into iOS's and Android's operating systems respectively. These apps allow consumers to pay daily transactions with their mobile phones, iPods and iWatch simply by touching devices on contactless payment points. The mechanism is straightforward: consumers only need to add and a bank card and associate this with the app. Google and Apple payment apps use near field communication (NFC) technology, which sends information from the personal device to the retailer's point-of-sale terminal.

Google first launched Google Wallet in 2011 and Android Pay in 2015. The former was a virtual wallet which allowed consumers to make payments and transfer money straight from their phones to online shops. The latter was a mobile payment service available on Android smartphones and Android wear-based smartwatches. In 2018, Google released Google Pay, a service free of any charge for consumers, merchants and banks which brings all payment services offered by the company under one umbrella. Through Google Pay, consumers can make purchases in stores using their phones, buy items in apps and on websites, send money to other people and add loyalty cards, tickets and coupons.[4] Additionally, Google has introduced Google Store Financing, which offers the opportunity to US customers to purchase selected items from Google Store with a monthly pay option.[5]

Similarly, in 2014 Apple launched Apple Pay, a mobile payment service, and Apple Pay Cash, a peer-to-peer payment service. However, Apple Pay is not free of charge. According to the *Financial Times*, in the US, Apple Pay receives 15 cents per $100 transaction, whereas in the UK, only a few pence per 100 pound transaction (Arnold et al. 2015).

Google and Apple take advantage of the interconnectivity between devices and operating systems to attract customers to their payment solutions. Apple Pay globally registered 270 million users (Loup Ventures 2018). In Europe, according to PYMNTS, 3 per cent of all smartphone users made a purchase using Apple Pay

4 Google Support website: *What is Google Pay?*, https://support.google.com/pay/answer/9026749?hl=en.

5 Ibid.: *Pay for your Google Store purchase over time*, https://support.google.com/store/answer/7166839?hl=en.

in 2017 against 1.9 per cent in 2014.[6] Considering there were around 258 million smartphone users in 2017, this means that approximately 7.7 million people used Apple Pay.[7] The percentage of all smartphone users making a purchase using Google Pay in 2017 was 0.9 per cent (about 2.3 million people), which represented an increase of around 200 per cent from March 2016.[8]

Facebook offers a peer-to-peer solution: Payment in Messenger. This service allows Facebook users to link their debit cards to the messenger's app and send mobile payments to friends through a conversation. In the US, at July 2017, 6 per cent of Facebook users said they used Payment in Messenger several times a day while 3 per cent used it once a day.[9] Since Facebook has around 214 million users in the US, this means that approximately 19.2 million people used Facebook as a means of payment for at least one transaction per day – a figure which increases to 25.6 million people if considering at least one transaction per week. To properly exploit its potential customer base, Facebook may develop its own crypto-currency, as hinted by *Cheddar* in 2018 (Heat 2018). Since May 2018, WhatsApp – a freeware and cross-platform messaging and voiceover IP service owned by Facebook – has launched a payment function in India. The *Financial Times* reported that Facebook may extend this new function to other markets (Murgia 2019).

Considering their access to a large and loyal customer base, it is not surprising that tech giants have an increasingly active presence in the payment service market. With their own payment services, tech giants gain a deeper interaction between their platforms and customers.

Techfins' mobile payment apps reduce the transaction costs of electronic payments (Surane and Soper 2018), but the key advantage for the suppliers of these services is gathering data on customer spending patterns and financial conditions S&P (2018): although payments initiated by Techfins' mobile payment services use credit or debit cards for finalizing the transactions, acquiring data on external purchases is great added value for tech giants.

6 PYMNTS website: *Apple Pay Adoption: Where Are We Now?*, https://www.pymnts.com/apple-pay-adoption.

7 Statista website: *Number of smartphone users in Western Europe from 2014 to 2019 (in millions)*, https://www.statista.com/statistics/494554.

8 PYMNTS website: *Apple Pay Adoption: Where Are We Now?*, cit.

9 Statista website: *Frequency of using Facebook Messenger Payments for money transfers and payments according to online adults in the United States as of July 2017*, https://www.statista.com/statistics/781802.

2.3 Competitors or frenemies?

It follows from the above that tech giants are targeting the revenues of the banking supply chain's most profitable segments. However, tech giants might end up being 'frenemies'[10] rather than competitors of incumbents: banks are in fact becoming the best customers of technology-driven services offered mainly by tech giants (IBM, Google and Microsoft hold ten times more Fintech patents than the fifteen largest banks in the world, according to Cipher) (Cobley 2018).

As banks are trying to automate their architectures in order to reduce operating costs, they will become more and more reliant on tech giants' services and products. A concrete example is given by cloud computing technologies[11] that have allowed banks to substantially decrease their costs (as reported by Anne Boden, Bankinter CEO, processes which used to cost $30 million today cost only $30,000 thanks to the cloud; see Detrixhe 2017). So far banks have turned to technological companies for their cloud-based infrastructures, with an expenditure forecast of more than $12 billion on the public cloud by 2020. Capital One, one of the first banks to massively use the cloud, is estimated to pay $150 million a year to Amazon Web Services (AWS) for renting its cloud-based infrastructure (Demos 2018).

Amazon (AWS), Microsoft (Microsoft Azure) and Google (Google Cloud) are the leaders in cloud-based solutions in the market – followed by Alibaba Cloud, Oracle and IBM (Smith et al. 2018). Synergy Research Group claims that AWS holds 45 per cent of the global cloud infrastructure market while IBM, Microsoft and Google have together around 20 per cent of the global share (Levy and Bosa 2016). The profits from cloud services are remarkable: $96.5 billion in 2016, predicted to reach $195 billion by 2020 (Levy and Bosa 2016). Amazon disclosed that, in the second quarter of 2018, AWS grew by 48.9 per cent, generating $6.11 billion in revenues. Amazon estimates that its cloud revenues will rocket up to $42 billion per year by 2020 (Novet 2018).

Tech giants are heavily investing in their cloud-based services and products, trying to catch up with AWS. Google has financed its cloud platforms, investing more than $30 billion in R&D (Bort 2017), while Microsoft is spending $10 billion a year building Azure data centres (Brengel 2015).

As stressed by a World Economic Forum and Deloitte report published in 2017, banks are becoming increasingly dependent on tech giants' services, the

10 The term 'frenemies' indicates someone with whom one is friendly, despite a fundamental dislike or rivalry.

11 Cloud computing is the use of various services, such as software development platforms, servers, storage and software, over the Internet.

only alternative being to fall behind if they reduce their reliance on tech giants (WEF and Deloitte 2017: 27). The growing dependency on technology is not only wrapped up in the cloud, but also rooted in the radical transformations that innovation is driving within the banking industry. Moving banks' infrastructure to the cloud will also unlock greater opportunities for integrating AI services and other technologies within their architectures. The cloud-based services market is a clear example of how banks are very profitable clients for tech giants, therefore raising concern that when entering the banking industry, leading tech firms may begin to erode this lucrative source of income.

It is not only a matter of cloud-based service. Tech giants are the market leaders at the frontier of innovation – from AI to blockchain.[12] In 2017, Amazon spent $22.6 billion in R&D – focusing on AI, machine learning, computer vision, robotic warehousing and more. Alphabet and Microsoft instead invested $16.6 billion and $13.03 billion respectively in R&D (Bajpai 2018). In AI start-up acquisitions alone, Google has invested $3.9 billion, Amazon $871 million and Apple $786 million (Krauth 2018).

According to CB Insights, IBM is the leading provider of blockchain-as-a-service provider, having 32 per cent of the corporate blockchain market. Microsoft enjoys 19 per cent of the market share while Amazon and Facebook are reported to be working on launching competitive blockchain-as-a-service products.

Although the market for technology-driven services offers the tech giants opportunities for growing their business, they may still have strategic interests in exploring an integration of banking services and products within their ecosystems. Tech giants are a new powerful type of ecosystem which aim at building an archipelago of interconnected products and services to become more and more relevant to consumers' lives (Dietz et al. 2017). Offering banking services then would simply be a side-effect to engage – and consequently gather more data – customers more frequently, using digital technologies to satisfy customers' needs (Berdak 2014).

As pointed out by Tirole and Rochet, a feature of digital platforms is to develop a two-sided markets model in which 'one side [is treated] as a profit center and the other as a loss leader, or, at best, as financially neutral' (Rochet and Tirole 2003: 991, Moore 2016: 14). If their target is to deepen their ecosystems and strengthen their customers' experience, they may work on low to zero marginal profits when developing their own banking activities.

---

12 A blockchain is a digital record of transactions.

2.4 Partnerships: a win–win solution

A recent *Wall Street Journal* article on the exploratory talks between Amazon and JP Morgan to launch Amazon checking accounts has revived the discussion on the mutually beneficial ventures of banks and tech giants (Glazer et al. 2018). Business cooperation between leading tech firms and established financial institutions is an existing phenomenon: several of the banking services carried out by tech giants are products of partnership with incumbents. This allows tech giants to extend their tentacles to every aspect of customers' lives and banks to access the large base of tech giants' customers – a win–win scenario. According to a 2017 KPMG report, 26 per cent of financial institutions are already partnering with one or more tech giants and a further 27 per cent are planning to do so in the next twelve months (KPMG 2017: 25).

This is the case of the aforementioned Amazon Rechargeable service in Mexico, backed up by Mastercard and Grupo Financiero Banorte. The advantage for Amazon comes from attracting more customers to boost e-commerce shopping growth through an alternative to credit and debit cards: the hybrid solution of a debit card loadable by cash better suits consumer habits in a market in which fewer than half of adults have a credit card and in which there is a strong preference for cash-based payments. On the other hand, Grupo Financiero Banorte's gains come from the engagement of new customers through Amazon's brand, expanding its customer base (Solomon 2018).

Amazon has successfully developed partnerships with banks in the US as well. The Amazon Prime Rewards Credit Card – which is issued by VISA and JP Morgan – offers 5 per cent back at Amazon.com and Whole Foods purchases and 2 per cent back at selected stores; additionally, it offers no foreign transaction fees and some travel insurance by default. The credit card does not technically have annual fees, but it is offered exclusively to Prime members who pay $119 per year for their Prime subscription. Where customers are not Prime members, they can access the Amazon Rewards Visa Signature Card which offers 3 per cent back on Amazon.com and Whole Foods. These credit cards are in addition to the Amazon Store Card and Amazon Prime Store Card – both backed up by Synchrony – which offer 5 per cent back on Amazon and Whole Foods purchases as well. While the former types are VISA credit cards and, therefore, usable anywhere, the latter types are cards which can only be used on Amazon.com. At January 2017, 15 per cent of Amazon Prime customers had one of the different Amazon credit cards – that means 21 million consumers (Trefis 2017).

These different types of Amazon branded credit card enhance Amazon's ecosystem, englobing customers with everything they need within its platform.

A Morgan Stanley report points out that Prime members tend to spend 4.6 times more money than non-member clients on Amazon.com, resulting in a deeper interaction between Amazon services and customers (Kim 2016).

In 2016, Amazon and Wells Fargo launched a 0.50 per cent interest rate discount on private student loans for borrowers who have an Amazon Student Prime membership. The discount is also available to borrowers who want to refinance their student loan. Whereas Amazon is interested in increasing the number of student Prime members, Wells Fargo aims at advertising its student loans (Mulhere 2016).

In 2018, CNBC wrote that Amazon partnered with Bank of America Merrill Lynch to expand its lending service, reducing risks and diminishing the liquidity directly allocated for lending (Kim 2018). This is just one of several discussions about Amazon and its partnerships within the financial services. Among these, the *New York Times* reported that Amazon has been in talks about partnership with JP Morgan and Berkshire Hathaway to offer health insurance products (Wingfield et al. 2018) and Ethereum World News wrote that Amazon will partner with Ripple to accept Ripple crypto currency (Tomzack 2018).

Apple Pay and Google Pay are also products of a partnership between financial institutions and tech giants, as banks need to allow the association of their issued cards with Apple Pay and Google Pay. However, concurrently, Apple and Google are providing clients with an alternative to credit cards. Despite potential dangers, many of the world-leading financial institutions have embraced the new mobile payment services offered by the two tech giants. In the case of Apple Pay, which involves a fee for partner banks, it is interesting to understand the depth of the penetration of the service within the industry. In the US, the ten largest issuers of credit and debit cards[13] – which account for 76 per cent of total cardholder market share – participate in Apple Pay.[14] In the UK, the biggest banks – such as HSBC, Barclays, Lloyds, Royal Bank of Scotland, NatWest and Santander UK – are part of Apple Pay's system as well.[15]

Beyond mutually profitable collaborations, there have also been clashes of interest between banks and tech giants. For example, in 2017 the four biggest

13 Such as Bank of America, Citigroup, JP Morgan Chase, Capitol One, Wells and Fargo, Discover Financial Services, Synchrony Financial Services, American Express Company, Barclays and U.S. Bancorp. See Harrow (2017).

14 See Apple Support website: *Apple Pay participating banks in Canada, Latin America, and the United States*, https://support.apple.com/en-us/HT204916.

15 See Apple Support website: *Apple Pay participating banks in Europe and the Middle East*, https://support.apple.com/en-us/HT206637.

Australian banks – Commonwealth Bank, Westpac Bank, National Australian Bank and Adelaide Bank – appealed against Apple Pay. The four banks were asking Apple to open its App Store and Apple devices' near-field communication controller in order to have the opportunity to integrate their own wallets (Smyth 2017). The Australian regulator however rejected the lawsuit, arguing that opening the NFC of iPhones would have affected the development of innovations within the payment system (Coyne 2017).

Following on the examples of collaboration between tech giants and traditional financial institutions, according to CNN, Apple will issue a credit card jointly with Goldman Sachs (Egan 2018). On the other hand, Google has partnered with four Indian banks to allow users to get loans via Google Pay (Iyengar 2018). Furthermore, in Ireland, Google and KBC Bank have launched an app which allows clients to open a bank account in five minutes. KBC provided the account while Google backed up the development of the app with its Android Pay API (application programme interface) (KBC 2017). In March 2018, Facebook launched a service which allows Citibank's clients in Singapore to check their balance account, credit card rewards and recent transactions through a Facebook Messenger chatbot (Harwell 2018).

Albeit all these examples of partnership represent concrete cases of a win–win situation for both banks and tech giants, they are plagued by an imbalance in the bargaining power, with the latter being favoured over the former. In fact, while it is true that banks can expand their customer base and access tech giants' innovation capabilities, tech giants may be able to improve their offer of banking services and products without exposing their balance sheets to risks and compliance costs. Moreover, tech giants are capturing clients and fees segments over which banks used to have a monopoly.

Furthermore, these partnerships may deepen what McKinsey describes as the 'four horsemen of the e-pocalypse': disintermediation, unbundling, commoditization and invisibility (Botta 2017). Since consumers will access banking products and services through the tech giants' platform, this will prevent the commercial relationship between banks and customers from deepening.

Smart speakers – such as Amazon Echo, Google Home and Apple Home Pod – will be participating in reinforcing this trend. These devices have started to allow clients to manage their bank accounts through these devices. For example, Capital One has developed on Amazon Echo a simple service which permits clients to track spending, check balances and pay bills with voice command.[16] The number of financial institutions which are exploring this business opportunity is constantly growing. In Italy, Banca Sella has launched its own service on Google Home which allows clients to check balances (last five transactions on debit cards) and to recharge debit cards (Ninja Marketing 2018). At the same time, these home smart speakers could improve the interaction between consumers and banks, enabling banks to have an additional channel to offer services and products directly from the home speaker devices (Wisniewski 2017). Once again, technology innovations can offer new opportunities for established financial institutions to enhance their business but, to fully exploit this potential, it seems that banks will need to partner up with tech giants, letting them enter deeper into the banking and financial sector. Nonetheless, these partnerships could produce negative externalities in the market. If tech giants can access personal banking information and provide established banks with data-management solutions – such as cloud-based services – they might have an incentive for the unauthorized commercial use of private information. In addition, if banks start to be involved in non-banking activities or change their core business strategies due to a non-typical dataset, they become vulnerable to new economic and operational risks.

References

Arnold, Martin, Andrea Felsted and Daniel Thomas (2015), 'UK Banks Put Squeeze on Apple Pay Fees', in *Financial Times*, 14 July, https://www.ft.com/content/02287f44-2a3d-11e5-8613-e7aedbb7bdb7.

Arora, Rohit (2017), 'Another Industry Amazon Plans to Crush is Small-Business Lending: Op-Ed', in *CNBC*, 16 June, https://cnb.cx/2JVnTJk.

Bajpai, Prableen (2018), '6 Companies Spending the Most on R&D', in *Nasdaq*, 8 August, https://www.nasdaq.com/article/6-companies-spending-the-most-on-rd-cm1004333.

Berdak, Oliwia (2014), 'Why Asking About Google Bank is the Wrong Question', in *Forrester*, 29 July, https://go.forrester.com/?p=44076.

Bort, Julie (2017), 'Google Spent $30 Billion on its Cloud and is Making Some Undeniable Progress', in *Business Insider*, 8 March, https://www.businessinsider.com/google-spent-30-billion-on-cloud-and-is-making-progress-2017-3.

Botta, Alessio (2017), *FinTech: How Financial Institutions in Europe (Should) Prepare for the Future*, Presentation at the Amundi Investment Day,

16 See Capital One website: *Alexa, Ask Capital One, What's My Balance?*, https://www.capitalone.com/applications/alexa.

Milan, 24 November, https://www.amundi.lu/professional/ezjscore/call/ezjscamundibuzz::sfForwardFront::paramsList=service=ProxyGedApi&routeId=_dl_NTlkMmRmYThkNTY5Mjk1YzZhNDNmZWFmOGIzMDRiMzQ.

Brengel, Kellogg (2015), 'Microsoft is Spending More Than $10B Per Year on Azure Data Centers', in *OnMSFT*, 5 August, https://www.onmsft.com/news/microsoft-spending-more-10b-year-azure-data-centers.

Cobley, Mark (2018), 'Tech Giants Leave Banks in the Dust in Race for Fintech Patents', in *Financial News*, 2 August.

Cocheo, Steve (2018), "'Amazon Bank' Is Already Here, Without a Charter or Regulatory Approval", in *The Financial Brand*, 20 August, https://thefinancialbrand.com/74543.

Coyne, Allie (2017), 'Banks Surrender in Apple Pay Fee Fight', in *IT News*, 13 February, https://www.itnews.com.au/news/banks-surrender-on-apple-pay-fee-fight-450874.

Demos, Telis (2018), 'Why Amazon and Google Haven't Attacked Banks', in *The Wall Street Journal*, 26 April.

Detrixhe, John (2017), 'Amazon Is Invading Finance Without Really Trying', in *Quartz*, 1 November, https://qz.com/1116277.

Dietz, Miklòs et al. (2017), 'Remaking the Bank for an Ecosystem World', in *McKinsey Articles*, October, http://bit.ly/2yPxI4h.

Egan, Matt (2018), 'Are Apple, Amazon and Facebook the Future of Banking?', in *CNN Business*, 15 May, https://cnnmon.ie/2J4CUU9.

Forrester (2017), *EU-7 Mobile Payments Will Nearly Triple to €148 Billion by 2021*, 12 May, https://go.forrester.com/?p=81516.

Freedman, Andrew E. (2016), 'Amazon Coins: What They Are and How to Use Them', in *Laptop Mag*, 27 January, https://shar.es/amkgKY.

Glazer, Emily, Liz Hoffman and Laura Stevens (2018), 'Next Up for Amazon: Checking Accounts', in *The Wall Street Journal*, 5 March.

Grosman, Lin (2018), 'What the Amazon Effect Means for Retailers', in *Forbes*, 22 February, https://www.forbes.com/sites/forbescommunicationscouncil/2018/02/22/what-the-amazon-effect-means-for-retailers.

Harrow, Robert (2017), 'Largest U.S. Credit Card Issuers: 2017 Market Share Report', in *ValuePenguin*, 27 June, https://www.valuepenguin.com/largest-credit-card-issuers.

Harwell, Drew (2018), "Your Banking Data Was Once Off-Limits to Tech Companies. Now They're Racing to Get It", in *The Washington Post*, 7 August, https://wapo.st/2B0LRi3.

Heat, Alex (2018), 'Facebook Plans to Create Its Own Cryptocurrency', in *Cheddar*, 11 May, https://cheddar.com/media/facebook-plans-to-create-its-own-cryptocurrency.

Iyengar, Rishi (2018), 'Google Will Now Help You Get a Bank Loan in India', in *CNN Business*, 28 August, https://cnnmon.ie/2N29ueU.

KBC (2017), 'KBC Launch New App to Revolutionise Account Openings', 7 September, https://shar.es/amkuzN.

Khan, Arif et al. (2016), 'Emerging Markets: Driving the Payments Transformation', in *PwC Reports*, https://www.pwc.com/gx/en/industries/financial-services/publications/emerging-markets-driving-payments.html.

Kim, Eugene (2016), 'Amazon Just Made Thousands of Books Free for its Prime Members – Here's a Simple Reason Why', in *Business Insider*, 6 October, https://www.businessinsider.in/Amazon-just-made-thousands-of-books-free-for-its-Prime-members-heres-a-simple-reason-why/articleshow/54706104.cms.

Kim, Eugene (2018), 'Amazon has Partnered with Bank of America for its Lending Program: Sources', in *CNBC*, 14 February, https://cnb.cx/2Hf5aTF.

KPMG (2017), 'Forging the Future. How Financial Institutions are Embracing Fintech to Evolve and Grow', in *KPMG Insights*, October, https://home.kpmg/it/it/home/insights/2017/10/forging-the-future-with-fintech.html.

Krauth, Olivia (2018), 'The 10 Tech Companies that have Invested the Most Money in AI', in *Tech Republic*, 12 January, https://tek.io/2mr3iNU.

Levy, Ari and Deirdre Bosa (2016), 'How Amazon Web Services is Luring Banks to the Cloud', in *CNBC*, 30 November, https://cnb.cx/2Uk5cTr.

Loup Ventures (2018), *Annual Apple Pay Review: Adoption Jumps, but Still a Long Way to Go*, 23 February, https://loupventures.com/annual-apple-pay-review-adoption-jumps-but-still-a-long-way-to-go.

Moore, Martin (2016), *Tech Giants and Civic Power*, London, CMCP Policy Institute at the King's College London, April.

Mulhere, Kaitlin (2016), 'Amazon and Wells Fargo Team Up to Offer Cheaper Student Loans', in *Time*, 21 July.

Murgia, Madhumita (2019), 'WhatsApp's Push into Mobile Payments', in *Financial Times*, 9 January 2019, https://www.ft.com/content/e045cdd2-0503-11e9-99df-6183d3002ee1.

Ninja Marketing (2018), *Banca Sella lancia il voice banking su Google Home*, 13 August, https://www.ninjamarketing.it/?p=515083.

Novet, Jordan (2018), 'Amazon Cloud Revenue Jumps 49 Percent', in *CNBC*, 26 July, https://cnb.cx/2OjuVpu.

Panebianco, Mauro (2018), *Il possibile impatto in economia e finanza dei GAFA*, Pwc Presentation, 14 June, https://www.pwc.com/it/it/industries/asset-management/assets/docs/impatto-economico-finanziario-gafa.pdf.

Panzarino, Matthew (2013), 'Amazon's "Login and Pay with Amazon" Service Challenges PayPal for the Web's Payment Business', in *TechCrunch*, 8 October, http://tcrn.ch/1bVDAFk.

Perez, Sarah (2017), 'Amazon Payment Nearly Doubled Transaction Volume in 2016, Added 10 Million Customers', in *TechCrunch*, 7 February, http://tcrn.ch/2knpQzB.

Protalinski, Emil (2014), 'Amazon is Killing off its Free P2P Money-Transfer Service WebPay on October 13, 2014', in *The Next Web*, 12 September 2014, https://thenextweb.com/?p=798892.

Research and Markets (2018), *Global and China Mobile Payment Industry Report, 2017–2021*, January, https://www.researchandmarkets.com/research/q2gr6q/global_and_china?w=12.

Rochet, Jean-Charles and Jean Tirole (2003), 'Platform Competition in Two-Sided Markets', in *Journal of the European Economic Association*, Vol. 1, No. 4 (June), p. 990–1029, https://www.rchss.sinica.edu.tw/cibs/pdf/RochetTirole3.pdf.

S&P–Standard & Poor's (2018), 'The Future of Banking: How Much of a Threat are Tech Titans to Global Banks?', in *Capital IQ*, 15 January, https://www.capitaliq.com/CIQDotNet/CreditResearch/RenderArticle.aspx?articleId=1980706&SctArtId=446588&from=CM&nsl_code=LIME&sourceObjectId=10396026.

Smith, Dennis, Lydia Leong and Raj Bala (2018), 'Magic Quadrant for Cloud Infrastructure as a Service, Worldwide', in *Gartner Reports*, 23 May, https://www.gartner.com/doc/reprints?id=1-2G2O5FC&ct=150519&st=sb.

Smyth, Jamie (2017), 'Apple Defeats Australia Banks over Mobile Payments', in *Financial Times*, 31 March, https://www.ft.com/content/8fb4f646-15bc-11e7-80f4-13e067d5072c.

Solomon, Daina Beth (2018), 'Amazon Launches First Debit Card in Mexico E-commerce Push', in *Reuters*, 14 March, https://reut.rs/2pbzsi4.

Surane, Jennifer and Spencer Soper (2018), 'Amazon Offers Retailers Discounts to Adopt Payment System', in *Bloomberg*, 2 May, https://www.bloomberg.com/news/articles/2018-05-02/amazon-said-to-offer-retailers-discounts-to-adopt-payment-system.

Tomzack, Alex (2018), 'Ripple's XRP and Tech Best Choice for Amazon to Go', in *Ethereum World News*, 15 August, https://ethereumworldnews.com/ripples-xrp-and-tech-best-choice-for-amazon-to-go.

Trefis (2017), 'Why Amazon Has Launched a New Credit Card for Prime Users', in *Forbes*, 17 January, https://www.forbes.com/sites/oracle/2019/03/27/

oracles-mark-hurd-the-cloud-represents-a-fundamental-business-model-shift.

WEF–World Economic Forum and Deloitte (2017), *Beyond Fintech: A Pragmatic Assessment of Disruptive Potential in Financial Services*, August, https://www.weforum.org/reports/beyond-fintech-a-pragmatic-assessment-of-disruptive-potential-in-financial-services.

Wingfield, Nick, Katie Thomas and Reed Abelson (2018), 'Amazon, Berkshire Hathaway and JPMorgan Team Up to Try to Disrupt Health Care', in *The New York Times*, 30 January, https://nyti.ms/2GuXbBp.

Wisniewski, Mary (2017), "Big Banks Hope Early Bet on Alexa Will Pay Off", in *American Banker*, 4 December, https://www.americanbanker.com/news/banks-add-alexa-skills-to-develop-voice-command-services.

Nicola Bilotta and Simone Romano

Chapter 3: Regulatory Framework: A Barrier or a Trigger for Change?

Since the 2007/08 crisis, the regulatory framework overseeing the financial industry has been greatly strengthened. National and supranational supervisory bodies have implemented stricter rules on capital adequacy ratios to reduce risks and moral hazard, making financial institutions more resilient (Gulamhuseinwala et al. 2015: 23). Regulatory requirements have traditionally constrained Techfins' expansion in banking (Williams-Grut 2018), discouraging them with high compliance costs and long and expensive bureaucratic procedures.[1]

The development of Fintech start-ups and the emergence of new third payment providers have however encouraged supervisors to rethink financial regulatory architectures. As an answer to the financial services landscape transformation, the European and the British authorities have recently implemented innovative regulatory frameworks – the Directive on Payment Service (Directive (EU) 2015/2366, or PSD2) and Open Banking, respectively. These regulatory architectures aim at improving consumer protection, enhancing competition and providing consumers with better ways to manage their money and data, resulting in new growth opportunities for incumbents and new entrants.

3.1 PSD2 between data access and enhanced competition

In October 2015, the European Parliament adopted the PSD2 and, by 13 January 2018, the EU member states had to transpose the new regulatory framework into their national legislation. Since then, banks and financial players have had to comply with the new rules until the regulatory technical standards release (RTS). This will probably happen in September 2019.

The PSD2 was developed to address some of the significant challenges from a regulatory perspective that emerged alongside technological innovations in the banking industry. The previous regulatory framework was not properly framing market developments and, as a result, several Fintech services and products were outside the scope of legislations. This gap between rules and market was exposing

1 For a more precise estimation of compliance costs in banking, see Farley (2017).

the payment chain to potential security risks, undermining consumers' protection in some areas and hampering fair competition.

The PSD2 harmonizes national regulations and institutionalizes new financial players, providing them with equivalent operating conditions of existing payment service providers. The directive has three pillar mechanisms to achieve its targets. The first is to require European banks to open their payment infrastructure and customer data to third-party providers. Banks are then obligated to grant access to customers' data to third-service providers when clients authorize them. The directive legally recognizes two different kinds of new provider which can access the data of clients' banking accounts: payment initiation services providers (PISPs) – which initiate payments on behalf of customers, giving assurance to retailers that money is on its way – and account information service providers (AISPs) – which give an overview of available accounts and balances to their customers (European Commission 2017).

To comply with the new rules, banks need to develop technical solutions to provide third-party providers and other banks with access to customers' account interfaces. Even though the directive does not legally bind banks to implement any specific technical solution, the majority of banks have chosen to use a dedicated interface, such as the application programme interface (API).[2] These regulatory changes affect the mutual relationship between clients and banks. If banks previously enjoyed a sort of monopoly over their clients' information, now clients get control over their data and they can decide with whom to share their information.

2 An API is a software intermediary that allows two applications to talk to each other.

Figure 6: Interaction model of payment services.

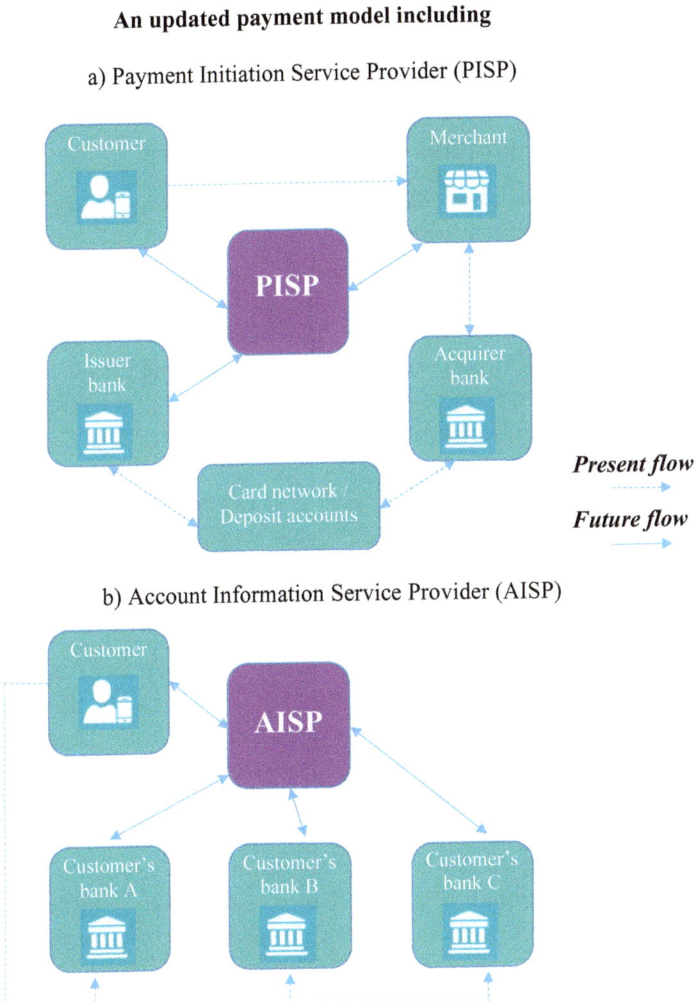

Source: Authors' elaboration from Light et al. (2016: 5).

The second pillar is to expand the regulatory purview in order to institutionalize new kinds of provider (PISPs and AISPs) which can build their services using banks' data (Art. 33 and 93 of PSD2). These new providers are not legally required to have their own funds, as opposed to fully licensed banks, because they do not hold clients' funds (Art. 35 of PSD2).

In accordance with Article 66 of PSD2,[3] the final pillar imposes specific limits on transaction fees, making e-commerce shopping and online transactions cheaper and easier. When buying online, clients will now have the ceiling on fees applied to their cross-border or national purchases (Art. 28 and 66 of PSD2).

3.2 Open Banking in the UK: a global pioneer

In the European financial landscape, the UK's Fintech industry has always been a step ahead, with London being the leading Fintech hub in Europe. The UK's Fintech development is rooted in the friendly domestic regulatory framework which tends to promote and foster innovation in banking.

In addition to PSD2, UK authorities have implemented Open Banking, that is, a new set of rules which has embraced and gone beyond the EU legislation.[4]

Firstly, the Competition and Markets Authority (CMA) forced the nine UK largest banks by deposit accounts to consumers and SMEs (HSBC, Barclays, Royal Bank of Scotland, Lloyds Banking Group, Santander UK, Allied Irish Bank, Bank of Ireland Nationwide, and Danske Bank UK) to comply with Open Banking's new rules before January 2018. The nine banks account for around 85 per cent of UK current accounts. Despite only three banks being able to meet the deadline, the CMA has marked a faster path for the UK banking system to embrace the new framework.

Secondly, the CMA has legally set standard APIs, using an open application programming interface, which needs to be adopted by all banks, differently from the PSD2 which does not state clearly how banks need to make clients' data available to third services providers or other banks. Technically, in the EU approach individual banks might develop their own solution to share clients' information, making usability very complex.[5]

Lastly, while the PSD2 allows access to client data only to specific providers, Open Banking may grant access to a broader range of third parties through its whitelisting process. Most notably, the CMA has recognized that price-comparison websites (PCWs) – which do not fall within the scope of PSD2 – will be authorized to access customer data (Doyle et al. 2017: 9). The new UK regulatory framework

3 In line with the EU Regulation 2015/751 (Interchange Fees Regulation, or IFR).

4 In addition to PSD2, the UK has introduced Open Banking which is a regulatory framework mandatory for the nine biggest banks in the country that integrates the norms contained in the PSD2. See Hughes (2018).

5 Albeit the PSD2 does not impose it, the trend up to now at the EU level is to develop a limited number of technical solutions in order to mitigate the complexity issue.

will then provide access to transactional data to more financial players than the PSD2 does, broadening the horizon of competition.[6]

3.3 The new regulatory framework: an opportunity for Techfin

The financial services industry is highly regulated, and the legal requirements represent the main constraints in banking activities. For these reasons the changes brought by the PSD2 and Open Banking can have far-reaching consequences for the banking market.

The key implication of the new regulatory framework will be the possible disintermediation between banks and their clients. PSD2 enables consumers to use third-service providers to manage their finance, increasing competition in the financial industry. Clients might be able to manage their money through different applications. For instance, consumers might use Facebook or Google to monitor spending or transfer money, while still safely keeping their money in their banking accounts.[7] Furthermore, consumers might use third-party applications to manage their accounts held in different banks (Barnes 2019).

As stated in a recent document by the Joint Committee of the European Supervisory Authorities (2016: 3), these changes have left incumbents worrying that technological companies might capture these profitable activities of the banking supply chain. Ralph Hamers, ING's CEO, has declared that the new regulations have 'opened the door to Big Tech entering the market' (Arnold 2018). Francisco Gonzàlez, executive chairman of BBVA, said that the uneven regulations under which banks and tech companies operate are an advantage for the latter (Arnold 2018).

There may be two principal potential advantages for Techfins. First, according to the PSD2 and in line with PSD1 as well, once having acquired an e-money and payment licence from any European country, third-service providers can operate in the whole of Europe – whereas banks need to obtain a licence from any single EU country within the EU in which they want to expand their activities (Hafstad et al. 2016). Second, bankers believe that there is an asymmetry in data-sharing rules between banks and Big Tech (Joint Committee of the European Supervisory

---

6 At the time of writing (this contribution was written before March 2019), the UK and the EU had still not found an agreement on the future of their bilateral relationship after Brexit. This uncertain scenario made difficult to elaborate any credible prediction about the future of the UK financial market and its development.

7 MuleSoft website: *How PSD2 will Revolutionize the Banking Industry*, https://www.mulesoft.com/resources/api/psd2-revised-payment-services-directive.

Authorities 2016: 3). Bankers have indeed called for reciprocal access to data.[8] The Joint Committee of the European Supervisory Authorities (2016) reported that it is important to bear in mind that enterprises from other sectors are among those using big data in a more intensive way – like GAFAs – and therefore regulations like PSD2 will favour them, helping them to strengthen their role in the financial services field.

Furthermore, bankers complain that if Big Techs get involved in the payments system, it will be hard not to see a deposit-taking activity (Arnold 2018). They finally pronounced that, despite playing the same game, banks and Techfin play with different rules.

While these concerns are not without foundation, it is important to stress that the new regulations may open new business opportunities for incumbents as well (Light et al. 2016). According to Article 20 of the General Data Protection Regulation (GDPR), which enables data portability,[9] consumers gain control over their personal data and they are able to require to an organization to give them a copy of the data they have previously provided. Consumers can then transfer their personal data to another organization, even a competitor, reducing information asymmetry and the time costs of switching between providers. Theoretically, whether they are interested or not, banks could access – with a previous consent – clients' personal data provided to other organizations, such as social media platforms.

Chitra and Shukla, in an Oracle Blog article, suggest that banks could potentially benefit from the PSD2's regulation, enhancing their platforms. If incumbents open their APIs to external developers – who may extend and improve the functionality of the platform – and to vendors, who could add value to the platforms for consumers, banks could lead the digital ecosystem of APIs, allowing traditional financial institutions to be more agile and create new opportunities in product creation and distribution while opening new revenue streams (Chitra 2017).

Incumbents could successfully implement a platform strategy with two different approaches. First, incumbents could build a digital banking platform in which third-party players, such as Fintech firms or smaller banks, can sell their own services and products, like finance management solutions. Therefore, banks could gain from integrating third-party services with their own and find cross-sell

---

8 To access banking data, tech giants need to have first obtained an e-money and/or payment services licence. In the European market, for example, Facebook obtained e-money and payment services licences in Ireland while Google obtained an e-money licence in Lithuania.

9 For a more detailed analysis of the new regulatory framework, see Scopsi (2019), a contribution that is part of the same research project as this one.

opportunities. Furthermore, banks could get fees from the third-party providers listed in their apps. Second, banks could join a third-party API marketplace in which developers could create services and products for them, reducing costs and time when building new products and APIs.

Therefore, PSD2 offers the opportunity to incumbents to improve the way in which their services and products are delivered to clients, embracing technology's changes.

References

Arnold, Martin (2018), 'Finance Chiefs Warn on Big Tech's Shift to Banking', in *Financial Times*, 4 February, https://www.ft.com/content/d9b3d79e-0995-11e8-8eb7-42f857ea9f09.

Barnes, Dan (2019), "Bigtech and Fintech Define their Boundaries in Banking Markets", in *Global Risk Regulator*, 8 February, https://www.globalriskregulator.com/Subjects/Reporting-and-Governance/Bigtech-and-fintech-define-their-boundaries-in-banking-markets.

Chitra, Tushar (2017), "PSD2: Threat or Opportunity for Incumbent Banks", in *Oracle The Financial Services Blog*, 2 March 2017, https://blogs.oracle.com/financialservices/psd2:-threat-or-opportunity-for-incumbent-banks.

Directive (EU) 2015/2366 of 25 November 2015 on Payment Services in the Internal Market, amending Directives 2002/65/EC, 2009/110/EC and 2013/36/EU and Regulation (EU) No. 1093/2010, and repealing Directive 2007/64/EC (PSD2), http://data.europa.eu/eli/dir/2015/2366/oj.

Doyle, Margaret at al. (2017), *How to Flourish in an Uncertain Future. Open Banking*, Deloitte, https://deloi.tt/2tRbby1.

European Commission (2017), *Fact Sheet: Payment Services Directive (PSD2): Regulatory Technical Standards (RTS) enabling consumers to benefit from safer and more innovative electronic payments*, 27 November, http://europa.eu/rapid/press-release_MEMO-17-4961_en.htm.

Farley, Peter (2017), 'Spotlight on Compliance Costs as Banks Get Down to Business with IA', in *International Banker*, 4 July, https://internationalbanker.com/?p=8130.

Gulamhuseinwala, Imran, Thomas Bull and Steven Lewis (2015), 'Fintech is Gaining Traction and Young, High-Income Users are the Early Adopters', in *The Journal of Financial Perspectives*, Vol. 3, No. 3 (Winter), p. 16–23, https://www.ey.com/Publication/vwLUAssets/ey-full-gfsi-journal-volume-03-issue-03/$FILE/ey-full-gfsi-journal-volume-03-issue-03.PDF.

Hafstad, Thomas et al. (2016), *PSD2 – Strategic Opportunities Beyond Compliance*, Evry White Paper, https://www.evry.com/globalassets/bransjer/financial-services/bank2020/wp_psd2/psd2_whitepaper.pdf.

Hughes, Marcus (2018), 'Addressing the Differences Between Open Banking and PSD2', in *Fintech Finance*, 21 August, https://wp.me/p6Xw2J-bEh.

Joint Committee of the European Supervisory Authorities (2016), Joint Committee Discussion Paper on the Use of Big Data by Financial Institutions, JC 2016/86, https://www.esma.europa.eu/node/82487.

Light, Jeremy et al. (2016), *Seizing the Opportunities Unlocked by the EU's Revised Payment Services Directive*, Accenture, https://www.accenture.com/t20160831T035645__w__/us-en/_acnmedia/PDF-19/Accenture-Banking-Opportunities-EU-PSD2-v2.pdf.

Regulation (EU) 2015/751 of 29 April 2015 on Interchange Fees for Card-Based Payment Transactions, http://data.europa.eu/eli/reg/2015/751/oj.

Scopsi, Martina (2019), 'The Expansion of Big Data Companies in the Financial Services Industry, and EU Regulation', in *IAI Papers*, No. 19|06 (March), https://www.iai.it/en/node/10163.

Williams-Grut, Oscar (2018), 'Apple, Amazon, and Other Tech Titans Could Threaten Big Banks in One Key Area', in *Business Insiders*, 17 January, https://www.businessinsider.com.au/sp-tech-titans-could-challenge-big-banks-in-the-long-term-2018-1.

Nicola Bilotta and Simone Romano

Chapter 4: Case Studies: Alibaba in China and Rakuten in Japan

As mentioned, Google and Apple have been very active in launching new payment services and Amazon has been engaged in lending money to merchants (Arora 2017). However, albeit lively and increasing, the expansion of Techfin in the Western banking industry is still a marginal phenomenon if compared with the Asian market, where technological and non-financial companies have already entered the banking industry, becoming proper competitors of traditional banks.

Acknowledging the differences in business and socio-economic contexts, which have a key role in driving the success or the failure of specific business models, the following paragraphs will look closely at what has happened in Asia. The case studies of Alibaba in China and Rakuten in Japan can provide useful insights to better understand and forecast the developments in Western economies regarding Techfin companies and their entrance into banking and the financial industry.

4.1 Alibaba, a giant from China

Alibaba is the world's biggest e-commerce market with more than 488 million customers recorded in 2017, bigger than eBay and Amazon combined. In the same year, Alibaba accounted for one tenth of China's total retail sales and for 75 per cent of total online sales (Liu et al. 2017). The giant created by Jack Ma builds its conglomerate on two e-commerce platforms, Taobao and Tmall. The former is a consumer-to-consumer (C2C) e-commerce platform while the latter is a business-to-consumer (B2C) online retailer.

Figure 7: Alibaba's ecosystem.

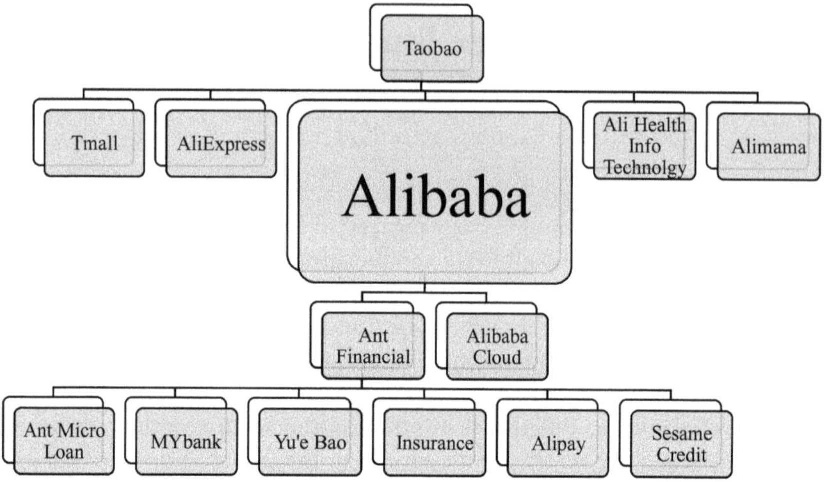

Source: Authors' elaboration from Ng (2018).

Key to explaining Alibaba's dominant position in the Chinese online marketplace is Alipay. Quoting Ying Yu and Mingnan Shen (2015a: 2), thanks to the protection that it delivers to its consumers, Alipay is the 'open sesame by which Alibaba unlocks the tremendous potential of the Chinese consumer marketplace'.

Alipay was the first Chinese online payment intermediary – an electronic payment system and a third-party online payment platform, launched on the Taobao platform in 2003. Nowadays it has become the most frequently used third-party online payment platform in China. In 2017, 72 per cent of the gross merchandise volume on Alibaba group platforms was settled through Alipay. In 2016, Alipay processed 175 million transactions per day (Aveni and Roest 2017: 3), 60 per cent of which were completed by mobile, for a total value of $1.7 trillion (Kapron and Meertens 2017: 6).

The popularity of Alipay goes beyond China's borders, with hundreds of thousands of merchants around the world accepting payment through Alipay (Lu 2018: 15). To illustrate the depth of the market penetration of Alipay, it suffices to say that it records 870 million active users globally (Lucas 2018a) while Paypal only has 267 million active users.[1]

1 See Statista website: *Number of PayPal's total active registered user accounts from 1st quarter 2010 to 4th quarter 2018 (in millions)*, https://www.statista.com/statistics/218493.

Alibaba developed Alipay emulating the business relationship between eBay and PayPal (Yu and Shen 2015b: 231). As third-party online payment platforms, they both represent a safe bridge between sellers and buyers. The guarantee function that both platforms provide to their clients is indeed similar, but their operating mechanisms are different: through PayPal sellers receive the money before delivering the commodity, while Alipay does not unlock the funds destined to the seller until the buyer has confirmed its satisfaction. Albeit this could seem an inconspicuous difference, it emphasizes how differently the regulatory frameworks in which Paypal and Alipay operate are: while PayPal had to avoid being classified as an 'escrow agent'[2] in the US in order to avoid complying with a specific regulatory framework, Alipay exploited the lack of the escrow holder concept in the Chinese legal system. Until 2012, when the legal acknowledgment of 'third-party payment solution' was officially introduced in China, introducing also better supervision over third-party providers, Alipay operated without having a clear legal nexus (Yu and Shen 2015b: 232).

Establishing an effective consumer redress system is a universal issue, but it is particularly risky in China due to legal inefficiency and higher moral hazards. When buying online, rational consumers need to trust that, in case of non-delivery or faulty goods, there is a reliable intermediary which will protect their rights. Thanks to the trust it has earned among market participants, Alipay has become the backbone of Chinese online transactions.

Over time Alipay has grown from a service to help clients buying goods from Alibaba platforms into a more diversified finance business. It has launched a mobile application that offers integrated solutions to consumers and small businesses for food, holidays and utility bills payments and it has developed an e-wallet which can be used in restaurants, supermarkets, drug stores and hotels.

Alibaba has increasingly loosened its control over Alipay to comply with the new rules on third-party payment services and in 2014 the online payment intermediary was rebranded Ant Financial, comprising the different financial activities of the group. The synergy between Alipay and Alibaba, though, is still the foundation for Alibaba's market development: indeed, Ant Financial used to give 37.5 per cent of its pre-tax profits to Alibaba (Alibaba 2017: 190). From February 2018, Alibaba has redrawn the agreement, jettisoning the profits share in favour of a direct equity stake of 33 per cent (Lucas 2018b).

2 An escrow agent is a person or entity that holds property in trust for third parties while a transaction is finalized or a disagreement is resolved.

Today Ant Financial is worth $150 billion (Weinland and Fei Ju 2018), implying that if Ant Financial were already listed, it would be the eighty-sixth-largest company by market capitalization in the world, overtaking giants like IBM, L'Oréal or McDonald's and it would be valued at about 50 per cent more than Goldman Sachs and Morgan Stanley (Wu and Zhu 2018). Ant Financial is estimated to end the 2018 fiscal year with 9.18 billion yuan ($1.4 billion) in pre-tax profits (Chen 2018) – an increase of 65 per cent with respect to the previous year. These figures are estimated using Alibaba's annual report as Ant Financial does not disclose pre-tax profits and revenues. According to analysts at Barclays, online payments accounted for 55 per cent of the overall $8.9 billion revenue recorded by the financial conglomerate last year, a figure destined to drop to one-third by 2021 due to the rise of Ant Financial's other financial businesses (Wu and Zhu 2018).

The cooperation between Ant Financial and Alibaba maximizes the efficiency and innovation capability of the whole ecosystem: data-sharing between the two entities allows for the design of better credit risk models and to develop tailored financing services using real-time data from sales, customer feedback, customer service indicators and other factors. Data are also shared to empower marketing penetration, providing a powerful and unique advantage for Alibaba to target the most relevant information to the most relevant users (Alibaba 2017: 80).

The strong business integration between Alibaba's online stores and Ant Financial also enforce mechanisms to mitigate moral hazard, providing for the possibility of closing down or suspending online storefronts and restricting marketing activities of people defaulting on loans made by Ant Financial Services or in violation of Alipay rules and regulations (Alibaba 2017: 187).

4.1.1 MYbank, a technological bank

In 2015 Ant Financial launched MYbank, a 100 per cent online private bank focused on inclusive and innovative financial solutions for individuals and SMEs. MYbank's technological infrastructure combines big data, artificial intelligence and facial recognition to speed up processes and make its systems cheaper: its cloud-based model requires much lower operational costs than the traditional bricks-and-mortar banking model (Millward 2015). This implies that Alibaba can have a much better view on the actual credit score and credit risk of a customer than can a traditional bank, as long as Alibaba can leverage the data and perform the right analyses. Each time an SME applies for a loan, the application process takes three minutes and involves no human intervention. When a consumer applies online or by mobile for a loan, MYbank's architecture will process 100,000 indicators exploiting big data, 100 predictive models and 3,000 loan strategies (Lu 2018: 22).

A loan application process has two steps. The first step sets exclusion criteria based on five factors. First, sales stability: a time series model is applied to predict the volatility of any credit candidate. Second, sales authenticity and illegal sales: a check is made on whether merchants have violated intellectual property laws or sold fake products, these being categories not eligible for loans – just like firms which have recorded self-trading or trade only with a unique counterparty. Third, logistics service quality, intended to verify whether firms have low standards in their timing or quality of delivery that would exclude them from credits. Fourth, customer ratings, as merchants need to have a minimum level of client satisfaction to obtain a loan. Finally, business network: Ant Financial accesses commercial relationships of firms to assess their credit-worthiness. Once a merchant has passed this first screen-checking, a second more comprehensive analysis of historical data on sales and financial information gained from Alibaba's e-commerce platforms is performed (Hau et al. 2017: 10–12).

Despite the high-risk profile of its borrowers, MYbank non-performing loans (NPL) ratio is around 1 per cent thanks to their risk assessment model based on big data (Zhang and Woo 2018).

MYbank annual financial statements show its rapid growth in just one year: from 2015 – when it started its operations – to 2016, the amount of net loans increased by 451 per cent, reaching 34.71 billion yuan ($5.07 billion).[3] The bank closed the fiscal year recording 315.54 million yuan ($46.17 million) in profits. Although this rapid growth does not help in assessing the sustainability of MYbank's business,[4] the figures recorded in 2017 confirm these positive trends: the total assets rose from 61.52 million yuan in 2016 ($9.02 billion) to 78.17 million yuan ($11.43 billion) in 2017; deposits increased by 53.5 per cent, from 41.19 million yuan ($6.02 billion) to 63.25 million yuan ($9.25 billion); and net loans grew by 5.17 per cent. MYbank's income statement also reveals an increase of net interest income (+54 per cent) and commission income (+224.7 per cent).[5]

3 Data are converted to US dollars using IMF's representative exchange rates at 31 August 2018.

4 In reading the high growth rates experienced by MYbank (and Rakuten Bank), its recent establishment should be considered.

5 Data are calculated by the authors from MYbank financial statements.

Figure 8: Increase between 2016 and 2017 by annual percentage.

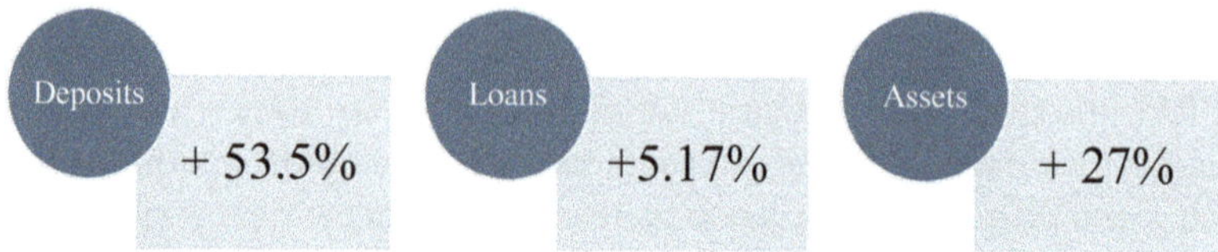

Source: Authors' calculation based on MYbank financial statements.

Zhang has expressed doubts about MYbank's model of cost-of-funding because the bank has heavily counted on borrowed funds from other lenders to support its loans. Accessing China's interbank market is more expensive than having normal deposits. In addition, the Chinese central bank requires commercial banks to have their interbank funding at under one-third of their total liabilities (Zhang and Woo 2018). In 2016 and 2017, interbank funds comprised around 56 per cent and 54 per cent of MYbank's liabilities respectively. Despite MYbank not yet having received any regulatory order to change its liabilities sheet, the bank will need to improve its cost-of-funding model, increasing its volume of normal deposits.

4.1.2 Ant Financial conglomerate

Alibaba's ecosystem comprises other Techfin businesses as well. Ant Fortune, launched in 2015, is a wealth management app that allows Chinese consumers to buy financial products from several Chinese funds – a sort of financial supermarket in which clients can purchase 900 different financial products from 80 financial institutions (Wang 2015). Ant Fortune can count on 25 million investors, 81 per cent of them aged below 36 years old, revealing the wealth management app as a great opportunity for younger savers to invest their funds despite having less money and no experience in trading (Meng 2016).

Through Ant Fortune, clients can also invest in Yu'e Bao, its own money-market fund. With more than 120 million users and $210 billion under management, Yu'e Bao is the world's biggest money-market fund. Ant Fortune users can also invest in Zhai Cai Bao, a platform that offers investment products such as loans to personal and SME customers.

All these products are supported by Ant Financial Cloud, a cloud banking and financial service infrastructure that has allowed Ant Financial to lower its operating costs. By developing its own financial infrastructure, Ant Financial has implemented a successful cost-saving strategy, avoiding the purchase of expensive external technologies.

A further pillar of the Ant Financial conglomerate is Sesame Credit, which offers credit-rating services to personal consumers. Alipay's users can get a credit score (300–950) based on personal shopping data, payment history on Alipay and other behavioural data from Alibaba's history. Sesame Credit's ratings have extensive applications: users can employ them to access credit loans from financial institutions and P2P platforms up to $44,972 and they are also recognized abroad to verify users' financial conditions, for example when applying for a visa in Luxembourg and Singapore (Lu 2018: 22–4).

Alibaba is building its banking expansion, exploiting its comparative advantages: first, a strong and widely known brand which has a user base of 450 million people; second, a high technological capability which allows Ant Financial to combine innovative products and services with lower operating costs; third, an accumulation of data that empowers the company to capitalize on the use of big data in banking.

In some business areas like payment and wealth management, Ant Financial is a direct competitor of established financial institutions. Alipay has de facto replaced credit and debit cards, allowing consumers to pay directly with their smartphones. Exploiting the defective regulation, Yu'e Bao is capturing market shares from banks' deposit business: while it can offer high interest return (around 4 per cent per year), state-owned banks are legally bound to pay 0.30 per cent annual interest for demand deposits and 1.35–2.75 per cent for term deposits.[6] When consumers choose to deposit money in Ant Financial's money-market fund, incumbents lose billions in direct deposits. In June 2017, Yu'E Bao recorded 1.43 trillion yuan ($209 billion), a figure larger than that of the total deposits of China Merchant Bank, the fifth largest lender in the country (Lu 2018: 24). Furthermore, MYbank targets SMEs and retail clients who are not served by incumbents, fostering financial inclusion in the country. Likewise, Sesame Credit is helping to reduce the existing information asymmetry between banks and consumers.

In the coming years, Ant Financial might shift its focus from financial services to technology services so as to escape the growing regulatory pressure of the Chinese central bank. Reuters has estimated that in five years' time, technology services will make up 65 per cent of Ant Financial's revenue, compared to the 34 per cent in 2017 (Zhang and Ruwitch 2018). Ant Financial would then offer its advanced technologies – which go from AI to cloud computing – to banks.

6 See Alipay website: https://global.alipay.com.

If this were the case, Ant Financial would shift from being a competitor of banks to a supplier of technologies. Whether – also after this forecasted shift – it would continue to erode profitability from banks remains an open question.

4.2 Rakuten, a global technology ecosystem

In 1997 the e-commerce marketplace Rakuten Ichiba was launched in Japan. Today it has more than 95 million registered users in the country and it has a market share of around 28 per cent of total Japanese online sales. In 2017, the domestic e-commerce gross merchandise sales of Rakuten were about 3.4 trillion yen ($30.67 billion).[7] The Japanese group has also expanded its online marketplace abroad, but the revenues generated in foreign markets are still considerably low.

Rakuten has become a conglomerate operating in a wide range of areas: e-commerce; banking; digital content; and telecommunications. Since the early 2000s, Rakuten has expanded its business, acquiring other companies (such as Infoseek Japan, Mytrip.net, DLJ Direct, SFG Securities and Minanno Shushoko) and developing its own services like Rakuten Travel and Rakuten Book. In 2014, Rakuten also purchased Viber, a cross-platform instant messaging and voiceover IP application (with 1,073 million registered users as at December 2018).[8] Globally, Rakuten's ecosystem can count on more than one billion unique user IDs (Rakuten 2018a: 12).

Rakuten's corporate strategy has been based on a one-of-a-kind member-based business model, establishing an ecosystem aimed at encouraging users to enjoy multiple services, all offered by the Rakuten Group. Rakuten's CEO Hiroshi Mikitani has acknowledged that his company is evolving from an e-commerce-centric model to an ecosystem built on data, memberships and a strong brand (Rakuten 2018a: 7). In this ecosystem everything is connected: as Rakuten becomes central in consumers' journeys, its clients have the opportunity to access its various services and products through a unique ID system. This is central to explaining the development of its financial and banking arms.

---

7 Data are converted to US dollars using the IMF's representative exchange rates at 31 August 2018.

8 See Statista website: *Number of unique Viber user IDs from June 2011 to December 2018 (in millions)*, https://www.statista.com/statistics/316414.

Figure 9: Rakuten ecosystem.

Source: Authors' elaboration from Rakuten (2018a: 7).

4.2.1 From an e-commerce store to a multi-business corporation

In 2004 Rakuten acquired Aozora Card, now called Rakuten Card, offering discounts and benefits if clients use it to purchase items in Rakuten's online marketplace. One year later it also bought Kokunai Shinpan to be able to provide credit card payment services with Rakuten Card. In January 2018, the number of card holders reached 15 million clients. Rakuten's 2017 annual report confirms the success of this synergy, giving credit for it to the prolonged popularity and impact of the Super Point Up (SPU) programme, which encourages users to stay within the Rakuten ecosystem (Rakuten 2018a: 18).

Thanks to the acquisition of eBank Corporation, an online Internet bank for payments, in 2009 Rakuten launched its own bank, named Rakuten Bank. The acquisition was aimed at improving the efficiency of the Rakuten financial ecosystem, allowing the Japanese group to offer its clients bank accounts connected directly to their Rakuten accounts: clients can deposit and withdraw money and cash-out their acquired points from Rakuten's loyalty programme at the same time. In 2010 Rakuten bought Bit Wallet as well, rebranding it Rakuten Edy, which issues the electronic money aptly named 'Edy'.

A concrete example to illustrate how Rakuten's ecosystem works is the 'Rakuten Card with Rakuten Point Card Functions' launched in 2015, an integrated credit card equipped with the services Rakuten Edy and Rakuten Point Card. The latter allows clients to use Rakuten loyalty points (Rakuten Super Points), gained by purchasing items in Rakuten's online malls, to pay in actual stores in Japan. Additionally, holders of the Rakuten Card receive Rakuten loyalty points with each purchase they make using the card. Today Rakuten Cards is the second largest issuer of credit cards in the country (Rakuten Europe Bank 2018: 3) and the first by shopping-transaction value (Rakuten 2018a: 6). In January 2017, Rakuten launched Rakuten Cards in Taiwan, reaching 370,000 cards issued in a few months.

Since its launch in 2003, Rakuten has issued around 1 trillion Super Points through its loyalty programme, worth around $9.1 billion (Yu 2018). To strengthen this programme, Mikitani announced during the 2018 Mobile World Congress that Rakuten is working on realising its own currency, Rakuten Coin, based on blockchain technologies (Lunden 2018). The new currency will also be integrated into the other services and products of the company. Finance Magnates suggested that Viber will allow exchange between Rakuten Coins and other official currency. Djamel Agaoua – Viber's CEO – confirmed that the company is working on launching Rakuten Coins in Russia in 2019, where Viber is more popular (Golstein 2018).

4.2.2 Rakuten Bank's development

Since its establishment, Rakuten Bank has experienced constant growth: between 2009 and 2017 its total assets value increased from 784.97 billion yen ($7.08 billion) to 1.71 trillion yen ($15.49 billion), a growth of 119 per cent.[9] Following this trend, financial products and services are projected to increase their share of the group's income in the future: the operating income due to domestic e-commerce is expected to rise from 96 billion yen ($866 million) in 2015 to 160 billion yen ($1.44 billion) in 2020, while the operating income due to the Fintech segment is projected to rocket up from 64 billion yen ($577 million) in 2015 to 120 billion yen ($1.08 billion) in 2020 (Rakuten 2017: 9).

At present, the Fintech segment already accounts for more than one-third of Rakuten's overall revenues: in 2017 the consolidated revenue of the group was 944 billion yen ($8.51 billion) of which (41.3 per cent) 390 billion yen ($3.55 billion) were from e-commerce activities and (35.2 per cent) 332 billion yen ($2.99 billion) from the Fintech segment (Rakuten 2018b: 22, 24), whose revenue share is continuously and rapidly increasing.

The biggest share (48 per cent) of the revenue generated by the Fintech segment in 2017 was due to cards, 22 per cent to banking activities, 15 per cent to securities, 10 per cent to life insurance products and 4 per cent to other activities. The synergy between Rakuten Card and Rakuten online market appears clear

9 Data are calculated by the authors from Rakuten Bank's financial statements.

considering 64 per cent of Rakuten Card's revenue was due to online shopping activities (Rakuten 2018b: 34).

Figure 10: Rakuten disaggregated revenue in 2017.

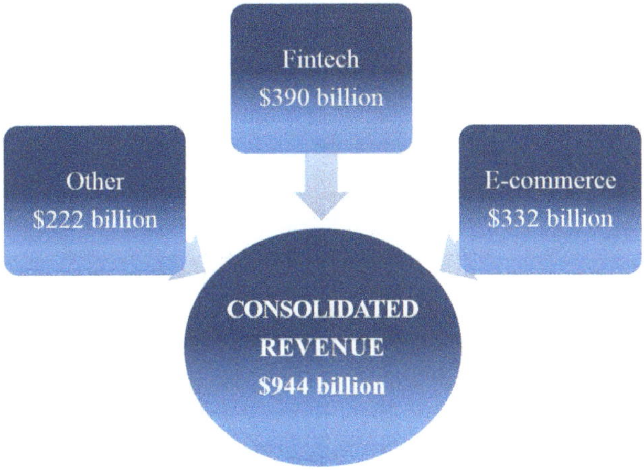

Source: Authors' elaboration from Rakuten (2018b: 34).

As shown by its financial statements, with the sole exception of the starting year (2009), Rakuten bank has always been profitable, with its deposits increasing by 131 per cent in 9 years. In 2017, it recorded deposits for 1.60 trillion yen ($14.49 billion). Total loans have increased by 577 per cent in the same period, from 94.70 billion yen ($854 million) to 640.96 billion yen ($5.78 billion). Rakuten Bank's return on equity (ROE)[10] was 20.32 per cent in 2017 while the average figure for the top five Japanese banks was 7.90 per cent. The situation was similar in 2016, with the average ROE of the top five Japanese Banks being 7.86 per cent, while Rakuten Bank recorded a figure of 19.25 per cent. The same applies to the return on assets (ROA) indicator: in 2017 Rakuten's ROA was 1.01 per cent while the average ROA of the top five Japanese banks was 0.45 per cent.[11]

10 In corporate finance, ROE is an indicator that measures how profitable a company is, calculating how much profit is generated with the money shareholders have invested.

11 Data are calculated by the authors from Rakuten Bank's financial statements.

Figure 11: Revenue of the Fintech segment.

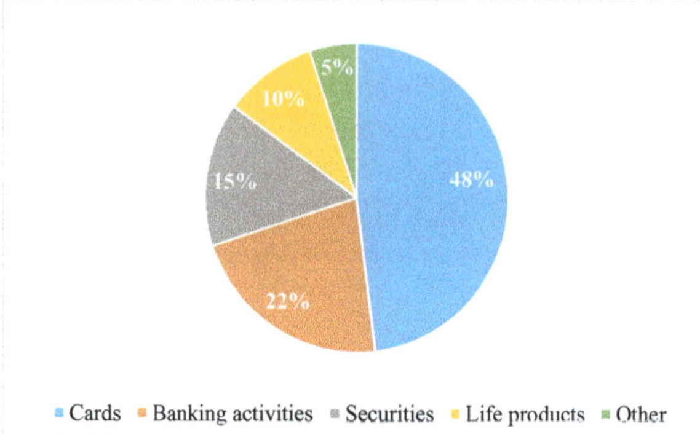

Source: Authors' elaboration from Rakuten (2018b).

The expansion of the Japanese group's financial branch has gone beyond national borders, reaching Europe. In 2016, Rakuten Payment Services – located in Luxembourg – was converted into a fully licensed bank. Rakuten Bank Europe has started to provide loans and receive deposits from merchants who trade on PriceMinister, the French e-commerce platform owned by Rakuten. According to Masayuki Hosaka, head of Rakuten FOS in Europe, the expansion is going to continue.[12] In 2015, Rakuten also launched a $100 million Rakuten Fintech Fund aimed at investing in disruptive, early- to mid-stage startups (Rakuten 2015), following an earlier investment in 2014 when Rakuten created Rakuten Ventures – a fund of $200 million – to invest in IT startups.

References

Alibaba Holding (2017), *Annual Report on Form 20-F for the Fiscal Year Ended March 31*, June, https://www.alibabagroup.com/en/ir/pdf/form20F_170615.pdf.

Arora, Rohit (2017), 'Another Industry Amazon Plans to Crush is Small-Business Lending: Op-Ed', in *CNBC*, 16 June, https://cnb.cx/2JVnTJk.

Aveni, Tyler and Joep Roest (2017), 'China's Alipay and WeChat Pay: Reaching Rural Users', in *CGAP Briefs*, December, https://www.cgap.org/research/publication/chinas-alipay-and-wechat-pay-reaching-rural-users.

12 'Rakuten Moves into European Banking Market', in *Finextra*, 11 January 2017, https://www.finextra.com/newsarticle/29972.

Chen, Lulu Yilun (2018), 'Ant Financial Annual Profit Jumps 65% Ahead of Anticipated IPO', in *Bloomberg*, 4 May, https://www.bloomberg.com/news/articles/2018-05-04/ant-financial-annual-profit-jumps-65-ahead-of-anticipated-ipo.

Golstein, Simon (2018), 'Rakuten Coin to Launch on Viber Messenger in Russia Next Year', in *Finance Magnates*, 4 July, https://www.financemagnates.com/cryptocurrency/news/rakuten-coin-launch-viber-messenger-russia-next-year.

Hau, Harald et al. (2017), *Techfin in China: Credit Market Completion and its Growth Effect*, paper presented at the ABFER 6th Annual Conference, http://abfer.org/media/abfer-events-2018/annual-conference/international-macroeconomics/AC18P1014_Ant_Financial_and_Growth_Effect_Paper_first_draft.pdf.

Kapron, Zennon and Michelle Meertens (2017), "Social Networks, e-Commerce Platforms, and the Growth of Digital Payment Ecosystems in China: What it Means for Other Countries", in *The Better Than Cash Alliance Research Series*, April, https://www.betterthancash.org/tools-research/case-studies/social-networks-ecommerce-platforms-and-the-growth-of-digital-payment-ecosystems-in-china.

Liu, Paul et al. (2017), "The Accelerating Disruption of China's Economy", in *Fortune*, 26 June, http://fortune.com/2017/06/26/china-alibaba-jack-ma-retail-ecommerce-e-commerce-new.

Lu, Lerong (2018), 'How a Little Ant Challenges Giant Banks? The Rise of Ant Financial (Alipay)'s Fintech Empire and Relevant Regulatory Concerns', in *International Company and Commercial Law Review*, No. 1, p. 12–30.

Lucas, Louise (2018a), 'Alibaba Revenues Rise but Ant Financial Makes a Net Loss', in *Financial Times*, 4 May, https://www.ft.com/content/6d756d0e-4f9f-11e8-9471-a083af05aea7.

Lucas, Louise (2018b), 'Alibaba to Take 33% Stake in Ant Financial', in *Financial Times*, 1 February, https://www.ft.com/content/009a1236-074a-11e8-9650-9c0ad2d7c5b5.

Lunden, Ingrid (2018), 'Rakuten will Roll Its $9B Loyalty Program into a New Blockchain-based Cryptocurrency, Rakuten Coin', in *TechCrunch*, 27 February, https://techcrunch.com/?p=1602374.

Meng, Jing (2016), 'Ant Financial Gears Up for More Wealth Management', in *China Daily*, 9 September, http://www.chinadaily.com.cn/business/2016-09/09/content_26748923.htm.

Millward, Steven (2015), 'Alibaba Launches Online Bank: "It's for the little guys, not the rich"', in *Tech in Asia*, 25 June, https://www.techinasia.com/alibaba-launches-online-bank-mybank.

Ng, Yoyo (2018), 'What is the Latest Alibaba Group's News – How to be a Part of it', in *Dragon Social*, 9 April, https://www.dragonsocial.net/blog/what-is-alibaba-group-news-how-to-be-a-part-of-it.

Rakuten (2015), *Rakuten Launches 100 million USD Global FinTech Fund*, 12 November, https://global.rakuten.com/corp/news/press/2015/1112_01.html.

Rakuten (2017), *Annual Report for FY2016*, https://global.rakuten.com/corp/investors/documents/annual.html.

Rakuten (2018a), *Corporate Report 2017*, https://global.rakuten.com/corp/investors/documents/annual.html.

Rakuten (2018b), *FY2018 Fourth Quarter and Full Year Consolidated Financial Results*, 13 February, https://global.rakuten.com/corp/investors/assets/doc/documents/17Q4PPT_E.pdf.

Rakuten Europe Bank (2018), *Pillar III Report: 2017 Financial Year End*, https://www.bank.rakuten.eu/files/REB_Pillar_III_Report-2017.pdf.

Wang, Yue (2015), "Alibaba Finance Affiliate Launches Fund Investment Smartphone App", in *Forbes*, 18 August, https://www.forbes.com/sites/ywang/2015/08/18/alibaba-finance-affiliate-launches-fund-investment-smartphone-app.

Weinland, Don and Sherry Fei Ju, 'Ant Financial Set for $150bn Valuation In Latest Funding Round', in *Financial Times*, 11 April 2018, https://www.ft.com/content/8af54946-3d73-11e8-b7e0-52972418fec4.

Wu, Kane and Julie Zhu (2018), 'Explainer: Ant Financial's $10 Billion Valuation, and the Big Recent Bump-Up', in *Reuters*, 18 April, https://reut.rs/2JUNQo9.

Yu, Eileen (2018), 'Rakuten to Release Own Cryptocurrency as it Looks to Enhance Loyalty Platform', in *ZDnet*, 28 February, https://zd.net/2FO3GRD.

Yu, Ying and Mingnan Shen (2015a), 'Alibaba and the Threat to China's Banking Sector. How Consumer Protections Are Providing Alibaba's 'Open Sesame' to Steal China's Consumer Market', in *FLJS Policy Briefs*, https://www.fljs.org/node/931.

Yu, Ying and Mingnan Shen (2015b), 'Consumer Protection as the "Open Sesame" that allows Alibaba to Crush the Forty Thieves', in *Journal of Antitrust Enforcement*, Vol. 3, Suppl. 1 (October), p. 228–241.

Zhang, Shu and John Ruwitch (2018), "Exclusive: Ant Financial Shifts Focus from Finance to Tech Services: Sources", in *Reuters*, 5 June, https://reut.rs/2JxjwTy.

Zhang, Shu and Ryan Woo (2018), 'Alibaba-backed Online Lender MYbank Owes Cost-Savings to Home-Made Tech', in *Reuters*, 1 February, https://reut.rs/2nvUqr2.

Nicola Bilotta and Simone Romano

Chapter 5: Political Implications

The digitalization of the economy has radically transformed almost every aspect of our life, offering cheaper and diversified services while providing producers with business opportunities to reduce costs and enhance revenues.

Digitalization exploits network effects, potentially leading to 'a-winner-takes-most-(if not all)-game' (Ghotgalkar 2017): ecosystems which are highly connected in one sector will have incentives to expand into other sectors of the economy, as nodes will link themselves with their core hub (Lakhani 2018). This explains why tech giants do not charge users when using their services: when buying an iPhone, Apple makes profits also from selling apps in its Apple store (Rochet and Tirole 2003), transforming users into consumers and (unaware) resources – what Ritzer and Jurgenson called prosumer capitalism (Ritzer and Jurgenson 2010).

Following this trend, tech giants aim at becoming a necessary medium between buyers and sellers, with the latter forced to join the platform if they want to stay competitive (Amstrong and Wright 2007), enjoying large returns of scale and network externalities (Schrager 2018). Furthermore, if tech giants want to keep extracting profits from several different industries, they need to increase the quantity of personal data which they are able to gather (Rushkoff 2016).

All these dynamics have raised concerns about tech giants becoming too big, too powerful, too intrusive and too rich for regulators and state systems (Rogoff 2018). This phenomenon is reflected in the growing dominance of intangible over tangible investments in the last twenty years: in 2013, for every 1 pound invested in tangible assets, 1.1 pound was allocated to intangible assets[1] (computer related, innovative properties and company competencies) (Haskel and Westlake 2018). Indeed, as highlighted by Wolf (2017), today the most valuable companies – the tech giants – own virtually no assets because what creates value is the integration of intangibles assets. Understanding this shift towards an intangible economy is crucial to identifying and addressing the structural

1 An intangible asset is an asset which is not physical in nature. Concrete examples of intangible assets are intellectual property – such as patents or copyright – or brand recognition.

issues linked with the digitalization of the economy, such as rising inequality and monopoly tendencies.

All these dynamics imply significant political repercussions, urging a rethinking of public policies to properly frame this evolving economic and social landscape. The possible expansion of tech giants in the banking industry – the main pillar of modern capitalism – further reinforces these trends. First, tech giants are already extremely powerful, with a structural influence on the global real economy. Their possible expansion in the banking supply-chain, even if only in specific segments, may make them too essential for economic activity worldwide, increasing further their economic and political bargaining power. Second, their business, based on the exploitation of technologies, intangibles investments and big data, is hard to legally frame and this fosters tax avoidance and profit-shifting practices. Third, tech giants have already based their success on data exploitation and personalization of products and services. If these actors were to gather data also from banking accounts and transactions, they would further increase their access to personal data, posing a potential challenge to liberal democracy. On the other hand, their entrance into the banking sector might foster the adoption of online digital identity outside banking as well, contributing to changing the digital space.

Albeit tech giants are increasingly aware of the social and civic power they need to embrace, they are becoming too big and too influential not to raise concerns over their political and economic unbalanced power.

5.1 Size does matter

The reach and scale of tech giants are incomparable to any other commercial organizations in the current global economy (Schmidt and Cohen 2014). Tech giants represent five of the world top ten companies by market capitalization,[2] with Apple and Amazon being the first to exceed the threshold of $1 trillion value of capitalization. Their market penetration derives from their dominant positions in key segments of the digital economy and from their further diversification. Google, processing 3.5 billion searches per day,[3] records 91 per cent of total online searches. The Android operating system – with its 2 billion users (Lee 2017) – registers a share of 76.88 per cent of smartphones worldwide. Combined with Apple, which has sold more than 1.3 billion iPhones since 2007, their share

2 See Statista website: *The 100 largest companies in the world by market value in 2018 (in billion U.S. dollars)*, https://www.statista.com/statistics/263264

3 See Internet Live Stats website: *Google Search Statistics*, http://www.internetlivestats.com/google-search-statistics.

reaches 97.26 per cent.[4] Amazon, with 310 million users and more than 353 million products sold (Hufford 2018), registers a share of 90 per cent of total online sales in five product ranges (Gesenhues 2018) and it records a share of 61 per cent of total English-language books sold worldwide (Jentetics 2017). Facebook recorded more than 2 billion registered users[5] in July 2018 while WhatsApp and Instagram had 1.5 billion and 1 billion users respectively.[6] YouTube has more than 1.8 billion users every month (Gilbert 2018).

Figure 12: Some of the largest tech giants and banks by market capitalisation ($ billion).

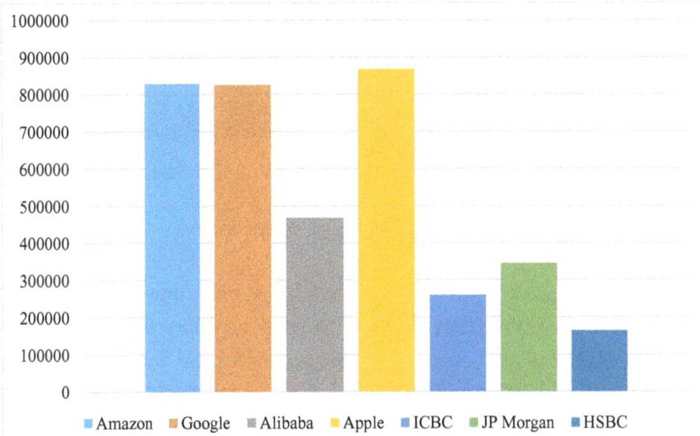

Source: Authors' elaboration from companies' financial statements.

4 See StatCounter website: *Mobile Operating System Market Share Worldwide*, http://gs.statcounter.com/os-market-share/mobile/worldwide.

5 See Statista website: *Most famous social network sites worldwide as of January 2019, ranked by number of active users (in millions)*, https://www.statista.com/statistics/272014.

6 See Statista website: *Number of monthly active WhatsApp users worldwide from April 2013 to December 2017 (in millions)*, https://www.statista.com/statistics/260819; and *Number of monthly active Instagram users from January 2013 to June 2018 (in millions)*, https://www.statista.com/statistics/253577.

Figure 13: Some of the largest tech giants and banks by profits ($ billion).

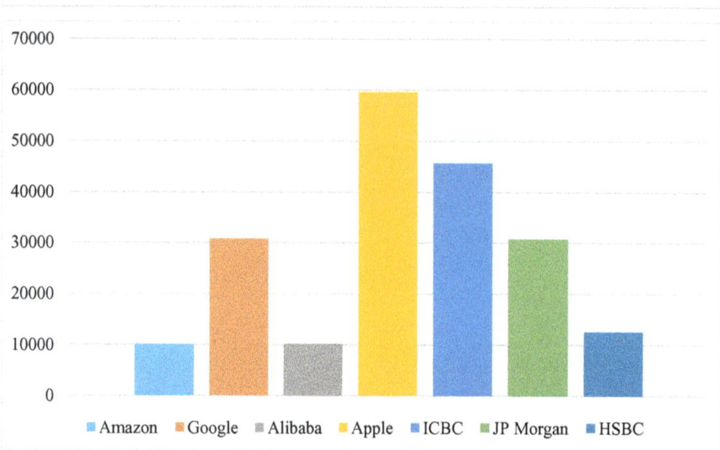

Source: Authors' elaboration from companies' financial statements.

These trends are increasing, with tech giants having become very different from what they were just a few years ago due to their capillary expansion: Google's online search engine is now only one of the technological activities of Alphabet, Apple does not just sell phone and laptops but also provides cloud-based services, Facebook has become a media and advertising company grounded on Facebook social media and Amazon has evolved into a giant marketplace embracing the most diversified activities.

Tech giants keep this prominent position by investing a substantial part of their huge profits in R&D and purchasing competitors.[7] Amazon, Apple, Facebook, Alphabet and Microsoft have made 617 purchases since 2016, spending around $128.5 billion (Whittick 2016).

The growing dominant position of tech giants has inevitably raised concern over a potential monopoly scenario. Public power has historically intervened to mitigate the risks of monopoly when unfair competition could damage consumers,

7 In 2014, Facebook acquired WhatsApp for $16 billion of which 2 billion was paid in cash and 14 billion in Facebook shares. That year, Google purchased DeepMind and Skybox Imaging for $500 million each, Dropcamp for 550 million and Nest Labs for 3.2 billion. Apple bought Beats Electronics for $3.4 billion, Amazon acquired Twiitch. TV for $970 million and Microsoft spent $2.5 billion on Mojang's purchase.

like the Sherman Act in the US, launched in 1890 to contrast the monopoly of Standard Oil which was controlling over of 90 per cent of US oil refinery capacity.

There are two caveats here though: consumers do not pay any fee for several of the tech giants' services and the Internet is characterized by natural monopolies as its ecosystems depend on networks (Wu 2010). Moreover, quoting Galloway, tech giants' power is only 'monopoly-like' because, despite having the opportunity, they have not raised prices, as is natural in a monopoly scenario (Galloway 2018a). Beyond the theoretical discussion, what really matters is to understand the implications of their decisive role as shaped by their size and reach.

French president Emmanuel Macron warned that these players are not just too big to fail, but also to be governed (Dalton 2018). 'Too big to fail' usually applies to businesses which have become so big that their failure would dramatically impact the whole economy, pushing governments to bail them out so as to avoid halting the economy. Traditionally this concept has referred to big players in the financial industry due to their fundamental role in the functioning of the real economy. However, today, in the unlikely case that tech giants may be forced to halt their business for reasons of external shock or constraints, the impact on the economy would be as disastrous (or even worst) as the one implied by the failure of a systemic bank, since their ecosystems have become crucial pillars of the infrastructures which connect the digital and the real economy.

Take the case of Amazon and its deep impact on the real economy. Connected to Amazon's e-commerce marketplace, there is an ecosystem of 1 million small enterprises which mainly rely on the platform for their selling. Amazon also employs around 566,000 people – being the world's ninth-largest company by number of employees.[8] Its market power is so structured that – as argued by Cavallo (2018) – it may have the power of affecting pricing dynamics and mechanisms.

Amazon's economic power dramatically increases its bargaining leverage. The Institute for Local Self-Reliance (ILSR) has found that Amazon has received public subsidies for at least 52 per cent of its seventy-seven fulfilment, sortation and other facilities built in the US between 2005 and 2014. For example, it received $61 million in West Columbia and $43 million in Baltimore (LaVecchia and Mitchell 2016: 64). States grant such high benefits because Amazon's facilities generate jobs and returns in taxes where they are located. A further example of Amazon's bargaining power was the race among US cities to gain its headquarters once the tech giant decided to relocate. According to Sage Policy Group, the total impact of

8 See Statista website: *The world's 50 largest companies based on number of employees in 2017*, https://www.statista.com/statistics/264671.

Amazon moving to Maryland would have represented an economic impact of $17 billion per year and 101,000 new jobs. The construction of the new headquarters alone would have created 50,000 jobs and $3 billion in wages (Sage Policy Group 2018: 3). Leveraging their impact on local economies to get public subsidies is a common practice among all big corporations – from car manufacturers to real estate developers. What is astonishing here is the dimension of the impact that is not comparable to other corporations.

Tech giants' financial power is at the same level as that of a nation-state. Only sixteen countries in the world have a GDP higher than $1 trillion, making Apple and Amazon's market capitalization bigger than 91 per cent of country GDP (Galloway 2018b).

Furthermore, technological intermediaries such as Microsoft, Apple and Google enjoy a strategic position thanks to their operative systems, making their role systemic and indispensable, as they own and manage the infrastructures on which the networks of the economy rely.

It goes well beyond economy: they also provide and shape the digital spaces upon which citizens increasingly depend (Manjoo 2017). Managing key networks of the web, they may have the political power to decide what and who gets a digital megaphone, and who to shut down instead.[9]

With a direct and sizeable impact on labour markets, social interactions and communication, technological transformations raise concrete political challenges (Manjoo 2017). As Ghez (2016) suggests, the power of tech giants does not stop at the market level nor at the company–consumer relationship: 'it is increasingly becoming political and even geopolitical by achieving a level of influence we never let big banks ever reach. In fact, GAFA's influence now stems from an ability to redefine a wide range of political and societal realities that are at the heart of today's global communities'.

9 For example, as shown by the latest presidential election in the US, Facebook admitted that it had not been able to filter fake news, affecting therefore the outcome of the election. As an answer to this issue, Facebook has committed to establishing (discretional) criteria for tougher control over fake news, meaning, however, the tech giant decides what fake news is. In another practical example, in 2017, the EU fined Google Shopping Service for 2.42 billion euro due to the abuse of its power in promoting its own shopping comparison service at the top of search results, distorting the market.

5.2 Fiscal and financial issues[10]

The intangible form of capital and the business models behind the success of tech giants fosters base erosion and profit-shifting practices, thus posing a growing challenge to fiscal authorities all around the world. The Organisation for Economic Cooperation and Development (OECD) estimated that the net tax revenue loss resulting from general profit-shifting in all OECD and G20 countries – accounting for 90 per cent of world GDP – amounts to up to 10 per cent of corporate income tax (CIT) revenues. Globally, this corresponds to $240 billion in 2014 only, or $2.1 trillion over the years 2005 to 2014 (Johansson et al. 2017: 8). Other estimates suggest values as high as $660 billion in 2012 alone (Cobham and Janský 2015: 24), corresponding to nearly 1 per cent of global GDP – implying profound political repercussions at the international level.

International law provides two criteria to allocate taxation power: 'residency' and 'source' (Vacca 2018: 3). The former refers to the location of the headquarters of a parent company and consists mainly of corporate tax, targeting the production side. The latter refers to all countries where single operating companies are located and the main fiscal instrument is value added tax (VAT), targeting the consumption side. In addition, fiscal contributions are also made via standard taxes for operating local services and renting locations, as well as employees' social security contributions (Jessop 2018). This kind of allocation splits taxation power between 'home' country, where a company is based, and 'host' countries, where a company operates.

This design works smoothly for traditional businesses based on tangible, physical assets but creates problems with intangibles, such as technologies or data, that can be moved easily across borders. A company is now able to extract profit from 'host' countries while maintaining little or no physical presence there, thereby being able to avoid one side of taxation. This becomes even more problematic considering the particular nature of business models based on big data. Tech companies collect information from the users of their services. The data are then used to provide targeted advertising and other services, which constitute almost all of the income for companies such as Google and Facebook. These profits are rarely taxed in the country where the users produce the data and view the ads, often unaware of the value they give away, so that 'host' countries are de facto providing valuable resources to foreign companies with no return at all (European Commission 2017). Adding more layers of complexity, one should not forget that

10 Section co-authored by Davide Ceccanti, Schuman trainee at the European Parliament and former IAI research inter.

the data are collected and organized using a specific software design and programming code, which are intangible assets, and stored and maintained in physical servers, all of which can happen in different countries.

Figure 14: Effective average tax rate in EU28: the digital advantage.

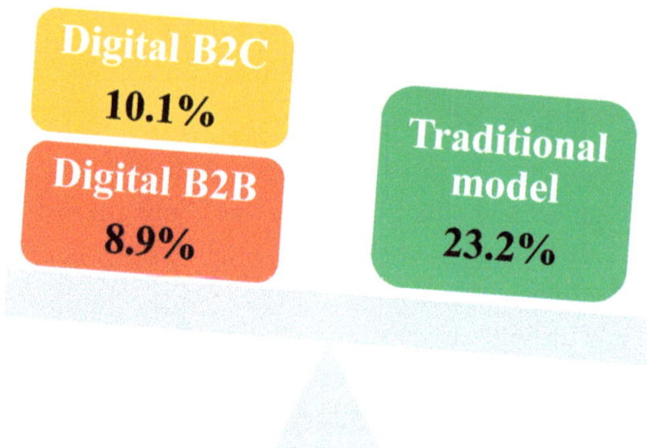

Source: Authors' elaboration from ZEW and PwC (2017).

As a result of the increasing importance of intangible assets and of the existence of different national tax rates, tech giants and traditional multinational corporations now have an easy time picking a country, normally a tax heaven, and make it the 'home' country so as to (not) pay taxes there. It is estimated that close to 40 per cent of total multinational profits are shifted to tax havens (Tørsløv et al. 2018).

According to some estimates, US companies alone possess over $1 trillion in overseas cash (Seguna et al. 2017), with just fifteen companies accounting for $776 billion in 2013.[11] This immense amount of liquidity is reinvested in the stock market, with a preference for low-risk US treasury bonds, which account for over $400 billion (Platt et al 2017). If these companies were to repatriate the cash booked offshore, as US president Donald Trump is encouraging them to do, they would have to sell all of their bonds and stocks, potentially threatening US financial stability because of the sizeable US treasury bonds sell-off. Then, they would have to pay the difference in corporate taxes between the countries where money is held and those they are moving to. Meanwhile, these investments mean that tech companies are already acting like investment banks. The size of the assets

11 For example, Apple is reported to have $111.3 billion offshore, Microsoft $76.4 billion and Google $38.9 billion. See Phillips et al. (2014: 11). For updated data, see Phillips et al. (2017).

they manage, comparable to those of JP Morgan or Goldman Sachs, make them key players of the global financial market, with the further issue that they are not regulated or nearly as transparent as banks (Foroohar 2018).

Profit-shifting operated by tech giants is a particularly serious issue in the EU. A small number of countries – Luxembourg, the Netherlands and Ireland – attract most of the digital giants, secretly negotiating even lower tax rates in what increasingly looks like the race to the bottom predicted by Cary in 1974. Moreover, an increasing share of new economic growth, being based on intangible assets, rewards capital, not labour, as underlined by Thomas Piketty (2014) in his book *Capital in the Twenty-First Century*. Income from capital is generally taxed at a lower rate than that from labour. The gap between the two rates varies heavily from country to country (European Commission 2018), thus encouraging capital flight. In the EU, free movement of capital in the absence of tax harmonization exacerbates the problem.

In 2014, Margrethe Vestager became the European Commissioner for Competition. She made the fight against preferential tax deals between member states and Big Tech companies her priority. Since there is no specific legal provision prohibiting this kind of behaviour, the commissioner introduced an innovation by considering the tax cuts as illegal subsidies, and thus a form of state aid (Larger 2018). Verstager managed to fine Apple, Google and Android for 13 billion euro, 2.8 billion euro and 4.3 billion euro respectively (Scott et al 2018). Relying on occasional punitive measures is not a structural solution though. In March 2018 the Commission tabled a twofold proposal. The first is a long-term initiative aiming at reforming the corporate tax rules so as to expand the 'residency' principle, including any significant company–user interaction through digital channels. The second proposal foresees an interim period with a 3 per cent tax on activities where users play a 'major' role, applicable to companies with global revenue of 750 million euro and EU revenue of 50 million euro.[12] These proposals build on the successful example of the VAT on non-resident suppliers of telecommunication, broadcasting and electronic services. The tax, introduced in 2015, forces providers to tax customers based on their residency, and has raised more than $3 billion for the EU (World Bank 2019).

EU legislation though often depends on EU inter-state politics. The French president Emmanuel Macron tried to champion the web tax proposal with the support of Italy and Spain, but encountered fierce opposition. Ireland, backed by

---

12 See the European Commission website: *Fair Taxation of the Digital Economy*, https://europa.eu/!XU63Yy.

notorious tax havens such as Luxembourg and the Netherlands, proposes to leave all the initiative to the OECD, which is conveniently unlikely to make significant progress.[13] Germany and Scandinavian countries are deeply concerned that such a tax could send a wrong message that Europe is opposing innovation, thereby losing global competitiveness (Brunsden 2018). This fear reflects the belief held by these countries that progressive reforms are only possible with the full agreement of the tech industry, made possible by the fact that tech giants have moved away from lobbying for mere self-regulation and recognized the need for moderate regulation, perhaps to avoid excessive measures (Scott 2018).

As game theory predicts, when the absence of coordinated (multilateral) action impedes an optimal outcome, that action by single actors leads to a sub-optimal outcome. This is exactly what is happening with regards to fiscal coordination. The Trump Administration in the US is taking the initiative to claim all of the profit generated by US companies worldwide. The UK had chosen to negotiate fiscal agreements (Sanger 2018), but is now moving towards a special revenue tax (Dickson 2018). Lacking a European solution, Italy is thinking about something similar (Valente 2018) while France and Germany are still working on finding a multilateral framework (Khan and Brunsden 2018). Tech giants on their side acknowledge the existence of asymmetries within the current taxation framework but reject new taxes on digital revenues and national-based reforms (CCIA et al. 2018). For instance, Facebook Europe released a public statement in 2017 in which it communicated that it will change its business organizations in order to locally record advertising revenues rather than recording them by their Irish headquarter (Wehner 2017).

The current legal framework based on 'residency' and 'source' is evidently no longer able to deal with the new context dominated by gigantic actors basing their business models on intangibles, thereby leaving countries to compete in a damaging race to the bottom. Just to make it clear, in Italy, Apple, Google, Facebook, Amazon, Airbnb, Uber and Trip Advisor paid 17 million euro in taxes for the fiscal year 2017, roughly the same amount paid by Datalogic – an Italian leading tech company – alone (Livini 2018).

Innovation requires increasing social investment and welfare safety nets to compensate the losers of the digital revolution but national states are less and less able to extract resource from the true winners of digitalizations. In these conditions, compensation is hard to achieve and the social implications of this

13 'Taoiseach Hails Improved Relationship with France', in *RTÉ*, 24 October 2017, https://www.rte.ie/amp/914733.

are already visible. In addition, tech giants find themselves full of liquidity in fiscal havens and de facto act like major investment banks without the necessary regulation, posing additional risks for global stability. Against this background, the international community seems unable to overcome coordination problems, resulting in a loss of global utility dominated by sub-optimal national policies.

5.3 Digital identity

The recent expansion of tech giants in banking raises concern over the key issue of digital identity, revolutionized by digital transformations (Boston Consulting Group 2012: 7) and tightly related to the accumulation of financial information. As noted by the Boston Consulting Group in 2012, people nowadays live a double identity: in addition to physical existence, people have a digital identity shaped by their activities in the digital world (Boston Consulting Group 2012: 7) and based on data floating around the Internet. People seem to be unaware of the extent and use of their digital data and, therefore, to have only partial control over their digital identity.

With consumers moving most of their interactions to online and mobile channels, digital data have become a precious commodity for the markets of identity: they have the power to provide accurate pictures of consumers' behaviours and habits that allow the offering of tailored products and services to individuals. Tech giants have been the first to understand the economic value of data, building up their business models on mining, aggregating and selling personal data for commercial purposes (Bria et al. 2015). However, this accumulation and access of individual data is raising concerns about who is controlling and managing them and how. The European Union has indeed recently approved a new regulatory framework – GDPR – to better frame the evolution of data management.

The concern over data protection is amplified when it comes to the banking industry. As online and mobile banking increases, the amount of valuable data produced by virtual banking transactions – and their potential value – increases as well. Consumers though tend to be more reluctant to share information with third parties when it comes to banking and to be much more concerned about privacy and security matters (this because financial information is regarded as the most intimate data of personal behaviours).

So far, traditional banks have been unwilling to provide third parties with the access to client data, clinging on security and privacy concerns. Nonetheless, with the described expansion of non-financial players in the banking market and the new regulatory framework (PSD2), banks are likely to lose their monopoly over clients' financial data. However, both incumbents and new players will probably need to face heavier rules when dealing with mining and aggregating financial data (Marksteiner et al. 2017).

Tech giants are interested in accessing individual's financial data to improve their profiling accurateness, seeking to acquire a more detailed picture of users' behaviours as a consumer and, at the same time, as a saver. For instance, Bloomberg reported that, after four years of negotiations, Google bought millions of data on card transactions from Mastercard. The deal aimed at tracking whenever and whether the advertisement online powered by Google resulted in a sale in physical shops (Bergen and Surane 2018). Albeit both Google and Mastercard guaranteed the privacy and the safety of the financial data, Google has started offering a service called 'Store Sales Measurement', allowing Google to anonymously match ads and actual store sales (Ramaswamy 2017). Clients have however not been informed that their banking data have been sold and shared with a third party, raising concerns over privacy and safety implications.

In August 2018 the *Washington Post* reported that Facebook proposed to partner up with some banks in order to access consumers' financial data – such as checking account balances or credit card transactions – and, in return, to introduce services like customer chat or account management on the platform (Harwell 2018). Facebook has declared that it would not have used user's financial data for commercial and ad-selling purposes but, following the Cambridge Analytica scandal, users may react badly if their banks decide to share their information with Facebook, being concerned that their data may not be safe and secure.

There are also concerns over the remote possibility that tech giants may be willing to find ways around the rules to empower their data collection, combing financial and non-financial personal information for ad and commercial purposes. The question is whether it is safe to entrust few platforms as the protectors of all consumers' information and whether the current regulatory framework is detailed and efficient enough to prevent abuses. To this end, Zuboff argues that a 'surveillance capitalism' is emerging in the global economy, grounded on mining, gathering and analysing personal data for commercial purposes. These mechanisms may be a challenge to democratic norms as they empower 'a ubiquitous networked institutional regime that records, modifies, and commodifies everyday experience from toasters to bodies, communication to thought, all with a view to establishing new pathways to monetization and profit' (Zuboff 2015: 81). Albeit Zuboff's mass surveillance approach may sound too alarmist, it sheds light on the need to better investigate the fragile link between growing digital data cross-sources accumulation and democratic principles.

A good example of the growing ambiguous interaction between physical and digital identities happened in 2016. According to the *Wall Street Journal*, Facebook developed a credit score system based on its social media to gauge creditworthiness. Albeit the system was rejected by the US regulators (Demos and Seetharaman 2016), the *Financial Times* reports that FICO and TransUnion, US major credit-analytics groups, are still exploring credit-risk models which use social media data in order to financially include consumers who have no traditional credit history and would be otherwise not be served by banks (McLannahan 2015). This was not an isolated case. In Colombia, the start-up Lenddo launched a credit card, backed up by Banco Colpatria, which assesses creditworthiness on social media data – like that from LinkedIn or Facebook – and the related connections.[14] The questions are: can Facebook's 'likes' shed light on people's psychographic details and how accurate would the pictures be?

Despite being a representation of a physical identity, digital identity has the intrinsic feature to be unbundling, as users can decide which attributes of their identity to share, questioning therefore the veracity of not fully verified identities (Segovia and Martín 2018 5–7). Whereas online platforms implement auto-identification mechanisms to sign up to their services, making it much easier to develop fake or uncompleted digital identities, financial institutions are today the identity providers which have the highest level of assurance in the online world, ensuring the veracity of their clients' identity for their online and mobile services. If, on the one hand, inaccurate digital identities may even have positive impacts in the social media or the Web, ensuring privacy and freedom of speech, on the other hand, banking activities and other types of online service require fully completed and certain digital identities to avoid money-laundering activities and to bolster security (Balani 2017).

The digital world needs secure and safe identity as public and private services available online are radically increasing, such as online healthcare records or employment benefits or taxation. This opens up business opportunities for banks considering their experience in managing physical and digital identity. A safe identity would be the passport to access the multiple online platforms which comprise an individual online ecosystem, instead of creating many separate solutions to verify users' identity (Finextra 2017). This strategy would allow standard banks to be still relevant in consumers' lives, strengthening and renewing their trust relationship with consumers. In Canada, for example, the SecureKey

14 'Lenddo Delves Into Credit Card Applicants' Social Media Data', in *Finextra*, 28 April 2014, https://www.finextra.com/newsarticle/26004.

initiative, launched in 2012, makes clients use their banks' digital identity to access government websites.

'The world of user IDs, passwords and security answers is a failed model. It's not a matter of if, but when, that changes.' (Yurcan 2016) Banks could therefore be the driving forces for this change. Yet there are many questions which remain unanswered: who will own the identity – consumers or banks? Should banks provide only their consumers with digital identity? Should public authorities provide citizens with a universal digital identity to use for all online services?

References

Amstrong, Mark and Julian Wright (2007), 'Two-sided Markets, Competitive Bottlenecks and Exclusive Contracts', in *Economic Theory*, Vol. 32, No. 2 (August), p. 353–380.

Balani, Henry (2017), 'What Faster Payments Means for Anti-Money Laundering Compliance', in *Journal of Financial Compliance*, Vol. 1, No. 3 (Winter 2017–18), p. 245–254.

Bergen, Mark and Jennifer Surane (2018), 'Google and Mastercard Cut a Secret Ad Deal to Track Retail Sales', in *Bloomberg*, 30 August, https://www.bloomberg.com/news/articles/2018-08-30/google-and-mastercard-cut-a-secret-ad-deal-to-track-retail-sales.

Boston Consulting Group (2012), 'The Value of Our Digital Identity', in *Liberty Global Policy Series*, November.

Bria, Francesca et al. (2015), 'Research on Identity Ecosystem. Decentralised Citizens ENgagement Technologies', in *FP7 D-CENT Deliverables*, 31 June, https://www.bl.uk/collection-items/research-on-identity-ecosystem.

Brunsden, Jim (2018), 'European Finance Ministers Agree to Intensify Talks on Tech Tax', in *Financial Times*, 8 September, https://www.ft.com/content/e44955ea-b376-11e8-bbc3-ccd7de085ffe.

Cary, William L. (1974), 'Federalism and Corporate Law: Reflections Upon Delaware', in *The Yale Law Journal*, Vol. 83, No. 4 (March), p. 663–705.

Cavallo, Alberto (2018), *More Amazon Effects: Online Competition and Pricing Behaviors*, Paper presented at the Jackson Hole Economic Symposium, https://www.hbs.edu/faculty/Pages/item.aspx?num=54935.

CCIA–Computers & Communications Industry Association et al. (2018), *Joint Industry Statement Ahead of the 28–29 June European Council*, 25 June, http://www.itic.org/public-policy/FINALIndustrystatementonDigitalTax28JunSummit-0625.pdf.

Cobham, Alex and Petr Janský (2015), 'Measuring Misalignment: The Location of US Multinationals' Economic Activity Versus the Location of Their Profits', in *ICTD Working Papers*, No. 42 (November), http://opendocs.ids.ac.uk/opendocs/handle/123456789/11202.

Dalton, Jane (2018), "Facebook and Google are Becoming Too Big to be Governed, French President Macron Warns", in *The Independent*, 1 April, https://www.independent.co.uk/news/world/europe/facebook-google-too-big-french-president-emmanuel-macron-ai-artificial-intelligence-regulate-govern-a8283726.html.

Demos, Telis and Deepa Seetharaman (2016), 'Facebook Isn't So Good at Judging Your Credit After All', in *The Wall Street Journal*, 24 February.

Dickson, Annabelle (2018), 'UK to Introduce "Google Tax" in 2020', in *Politico*, 29 October, https://www.politico.eu/article/uk-to-bring-in-digital-services-tax-in-2020.

European Commission (2017), *A Fair and Efficient Tax System in the European Union for the Digital Single Market*, COM/2017/547, 21 September, https://eur-lex.europa.eu/legal-content/EN/TXT/?uri=CELEX:52017DC0547.

European Commission (2018), *Taxation Trends in the European Union. Data for the EU Member States, Iceland and Norway. 2018 Edition*, Luxembourg, Publications Office of the European Union, https://doi.org/10.2778/025314.

Finextra (2017), *The Role of Digital Identity in the Future of Banking*, London, Finextra Research, October.

Foroohar, Rana (2018), 'Tech Companies are the New Investment Banks', in *Financial Times*, 11 February, https://www.ft.com/content/0ee3bef8-0d87-11e8-8eb7-42f857ea9f09.

Galloway, Scott (2018a), 'Silicon Valley's Tax-Avoiding, Job-Killing, Soul-Sucking Machine', in *Esquire*, March, p. 124–136, https://classic.esquire.com/article/2018/3/1/silicon-valleys-tax-avoiding-job-killing-soul-sucking-machine.

Galloway, Scott (2018b), 'Yay, Capitalism', in *The Daily Gartner L2*, 3 August, https://www.l2inc.com/?p=203746.

Gesenhues, Amy (2018), 'Amazon Owns More than 90% Market Share Across 5 Different Product Categories', in *Marketing Land*, 31 May, https://mklnd.com/2U7luQs.

Ghez, Jeremy (2016), 'Why U.S. Tech Giants Might Not Dominate the World After All', in *Forbes*, 16 November, https://www.forbes.com/sites/hecparis/2016/11/16/why-us-tech-giants-might-not-dominate-the-world-after-all.

Ghotgalkar, Varun et al. (2017), 'How the Digital Economy is Changing Corporate Pricing and Inflation', in *AXA Investment Research*, 22 August, https://www.axa-im.com/documents/20195/859236/How+the+digital+econom

y+is+changing+corporate+pricing+and+inflation+20170822+en/0e395a9f-7e76-7468-c807-9a968b3abefb.

Gilbert, Ben (2018), "YouTube Now Has Over 1.8 Billion Users Every Month, Within Spitting Distance of Facebook's 2 Billion", in *Business Insider*, 4 May 2018, http://markets.businessinsider.com/news/1023392460.

Harwell, Drew (2018), 'Your Banking Data was Once Off-Limits to Tech Companies. Now They're Racing to Get It', in *The Washington Post*, 7 August, https://www.washingtonpost.com/technology/2018/08/07/your-banking-data-was-once-off-limits-tech-companies-now-theyre-racing-get-it.

Haskel, Jonathan and Stian Westlake (2018), 'Productivity and Secular Stagnation in the Intangible Economy', in *VOX*, 31 May, https://voxeu.org/node/62502.

Hufford, Jillian (2018), 'Amazon Statistics: Need To Know Numbers about Amazon', in *nChannel*, 24 January, https://www.nchannel.com/?p=15640.

Jentetics, Kinga (2017), 'Amazon Ebook Market Share 2017 – Is It Big Enough?', in *PublishDrive*, 4 January, https://publishdrive.com/amazon-ebook-market-share.

Jessop, Julian (2018), 'Supervising the Tech Giants. Markets Will Do a Better Job Than State Regulation', in *IEA Current Controversies*, No. 56 (January), https://iea.org.uk/?p=26026.

Johansson, Åsa et al. (2017), 'Tax Planning by Multinational Firms: Firm Level Evidence From a Cross Country Database', in *OECD Economics Department Working Papers*, No. 1355 (February), https://dx.doi.org/10.1787/9ea89b4d-en.

Khan, Mahreen and Jim Brunsden (2018), "France and Germany Abandon Plans for EU Digital Tax", in *Financial Times*, 4 December, https://www.ft.com/content/fc7330d4-f730-11e8-af46-2022a0b02a6c.

Lakhani, Karim (2018), 'The Era of the Hub Economy', in *Cutter Business Technology Journal*, Vol. 31, No. 1 (February), https://www.cutter.com/article/era-hub-economy-498446.

Larger, Thibault (2018), 'EU's Vestager Examines Facebook for Potential Tax Probe', in *Politico*, 11 August, https://www.politico.eu/article/eus-vestager-examines-facebook-for-potential-tax-probe.

LaVecchia, Olivia and Stacy Mitchell (2016), 'Amazon's Stranglehold: How the Company's Tightening Grip is Stifling Competition, Eroding Jobs, and Threatening Communities', in ILSR Reports, November, https://ilsr.org/?p=44979.

Lee, Tyler (2017), 'Android Now Has 2 Billion Monthly Active Users', in *Ubergizmo*, 17 May, https://www.ubergizmo.com/?p=281376.

Livini, Ettore (2018), 'Affari e profitti record ma dal club dei trilionari solo 14 milioni di tasse', in *Repubblica*, 4 August.

Manjoo, Farhad (2017), 'The Upside of Being Ruled by the Five Tech Giants', in *The New York Times*, 1 November, https://nyti.ms/2z2QbIE.

Marksteiner, Lukas et al. (2017), 'General Data Protection Regulation. A Comprehensive Approach to Meet Requirements in a Digitalized World', in *Banking Hub*, 25 January, https://www.bankinghub.eu/?p=6809.

McLannahan, Ben (2015), 'Being "Wasted" on Facebook May Damage Your Credit Score', in *Financial Times*, 15 October, https://www.ft.com/content/d6daedee-706a-11e5-9b9e-690fdae72044.

Phillips, Richard, Steve Wamhoff and Dan Smith (2014), *Offshore Shell Games 2014. The Use of Offshore Tax Havens by Fortune 500 Companies*, Institute on Taxation and Economic Policy and U.S. PIRG Education Fund, June, https://www.ctj.org/offshore-shell-games-2014.

Phillips, Richard et al. (2017), *Offshore Shell Games 2017. The Use of Offshore Tax Havens by Fortune 500 Companies*, Institute on Taxation and Economic Policy and U.S. PIRG Education Fund, October, https://uspirg.org/sites/pirg/files/cpn/USN-011218-B2-REPORT/Offshore-Shell-Games_3.html.

Piketty, Thomas (2014), *Capital in the Twenty-First Century*, Cambridge, The Belknap Press of Harvard University Press.

Platt, Eric, Nicole Bullock and Alexandra Scaggs (2017), 'US Companies Transformed into 800lb Gorilla in Bond Market', in *Financial Times*, 12 September, https://www.ft.com/content/46027dd2-8f6c-11e7-9084-d0c17942ba93.

Ritzer, George and Nathan Jurgenson (2010), 'Production, Consumption, Prosumption: The Nature of Capitalism in the Age of the Digital "Prosumer"', in *Journal of Consumer Culture*, Vol. 10, No. 1 (March), p. 13–36.

Ramaswamy, Sridhar (2017), 'Powering Ads and Analytics Innovations with Machine Learning', in *Google Marketing Platform Blog*, 23 May, https://www.blog.google/products/marketingplatform/360/powering-ads-analytics-innovations-with-machine-learning-xp.

Rochet, Jean-Charles and Jean Tirole (2003), 'Platform Competition in Two-Sided Markets', in *Journal of the European Economic Association*, Vol. 1, No. 4 (June), p. 990–1029, https://www.rchss.sinica.edu.tw/cibs/pdf/RochetTirole3.pdf.

Rogoff, Kenneth (2018), "Big Tech is a Big Problem", in *Project Syndicate*, 2 July, http://prosyn.org/04u7Olw.

Rushkoff, Douglas (2016), *Throwing Rocks at the Google Bus. How Growth Became the Enemy of Prosperity*, New York, Portfolio/Penguin.

Sage Policy Group (2018), *Economic Contributions of the Potential Amazon HQ2 in Maryland*, Report submitted to the State of Maryland & Montgomery County, February, http://commerce.maryland.gov/commerce/Documents/sage-mo-co.pdf.

Sanger, Chris (2018), 'The UK is Gunning for More Tax from Big Tech. But It's Not So Easy', in *Wired*, 26 February, https://www.wired.co.uk/article/turnover-tax-tech-companies-web-tax.

Schrager, Allison (2018), 'A Nobel-Winning Economist's Guide to Taming Tech Monopolies', in *Quartz*, 27 June, https://qz.com/1310266.

Schmidt, Eric and Jared Cohen (2014), *The New Digital Age: Transforming Nations, Businesses and Our Lives*, New York, Vintage Books.

Scott, Mark (2018), 'How Big Tech Learned to Love Regulation', in *Politico*, 11 November, https://www.politico.eu/article/google-facebook-amazon-regulation-europe-washington-brussels-privacy-competition-tax-vestager.

Scott, Mark, Simon van Dorpe and Thibault Larger (2018), 'With Record Antitrust Fine, Europe Lands Blow Against Google', in *Politico*, 7 August, https://www.politico.eu/article/google-to-be-fined-e4-3-billion-in-android-antitrust-decision-2.

Segovia Domingo, Ana Isabel and Álvaro Martín Enríquez (2018), 'Digital Identity: The Current State of Affairs', in *BBVA Working Papers*, No. 18/01 (February), https://www.bbvaresearch.com/?p=196541.

Seguna, Sal et al. (2017), 'The Bottom Line: What Tax Reform Means for Your Company', in *Credit Suisse Corporate Insights*, 2017 Second Quarter, https://www.credit-suisse.com/media/assets/microsite/docs/corporate-insights/corporate-insights-q2-2017.pdf.

Tørsløv, Thomas R., Ludvig S. Wier and Gabriel Zucman (2018), 'The Missing Profits of Nations', in *NBER Working Papers*, No. 24701 (June), http://gabriel-zucman.eu/?p=1175.

Vacca, Ivan (2018), 'Web Tax: The Real Question is Not "What to Tax" but "Who Can Tax"', in *Assonime Position Papers*, No. 1/2018 (September), http://www.assonime.it/attivita-editoriale/position-papers/Documents/PP108Eng.pdf.

Valente, Piergiorgio (2018), 'Italy/International – The Italian Web Tax from a National and International Perspective', in *European Taxation*, Vol. 58, No. 5, May, p. 186–190.

Wehner, Dave (2017), 'Moving to a Local Selling Model', in *Facebook Newsroom*, 12 December, https://wp.me/p4eLrC-2r8.

Whittick, Simon (2016), "We Visualized Acquisitions by the Big Five Tech Companies Since 1985, Here's What We Learned", in *Geckoboard Blog*, 25 October, https://www.geckoboard.com/blog/acquisitions-mergers-big-five-tech-companies.

Wolf, Martin (2017), 'The Challenges of a Disembodied Economy', in *Financial Times*, 28 November, https://www.ft.com/content/a01e7262-d35a-11e7-a303-9060cb1e5f44.

World Bank (2019), *World Development Report 2019: The Changing Nature of Work*, Washington, World Bank, http://www.worldbank.org/en/publication/wdr2019.

Wu, Tim (2010), 'In the Grip of the New Monopolists', in *The Wall Street Journal*, 13 November.

Yurcan, Bryan (2016), 'The Future of Digital Identity is Up To Banks', in *American Banker*, 27 March, https://www.americanbanker.com/news/the-future-of-digital-identity-is-up-to-banks.

ZEW and PwC (2017), *Digital Tax Index 2017: Locational Tax Attractiveness for Digital Business Models*, May.

Zuboff, Shoshana (2015), 'Big Other: Surveillance Capitalism and the Prospects of an Information Civilization', in *Journal of Information Technology*, Vol. 30, No. 1 (April), p. 75–89.

Part Two: Focus

Filippo Renga, Laura Grassi and Nadir Snouno[1]

Focus 1: The Fintech Ecosystem: An Italian Perspective

Digitalization has brought substantial change to the world of banking and finance. Changes that have been happening for over a decade already, with consequences that we still cannot fully comprehend on all fronts, such as the decline in the use of cash, the reduction in the number of bank branches and bank employees, the role of new channels for communicating with clients, and the digitalization of banking and financial activity.

The digitalization of the financial system is not, therefore, something that has emerged only in recent years, but we are experiencing profound changes to financial and banking business models, where information has become not just the data at the base of every service offered, but often also the very source of competitive advantage, and partly in the speed at which changes are continuously emerging, including a continuous redrawing of the lines of competition. Several digital pressures, both internal and external, are significantly changing financial institutions, and banks in particular.

If we consider the external pressures, the Observatory considers the following three push factors to be particularly significant.

First, the ambition of technology companies in the financial sphere. The experience of PayPal and some mobile banking and mobile payment solutions in unbanked markets, such as in China, have shown how some stakeholders totally removed from the financial market can have a significant impact on some segments of financial services. This is corroborated, for example, by the fifty-one large international companies from non-financial sectors (retail, telecom, consumer electronics, and so on) that offer over 120 solutions between banking and insurance.

Second, the vitality of Fintech startups. It is already documented that funding received by startups in the Fintech sector are in the tens of billions of dollars: we recorded over $25 billion for the period 2014–17. Few, however, have turned out to be real disruptors of market components or have managed to become market

1 Filippo Renga is Research Director of the Fintech & Insurtech Observatory, School of Management – Politecnico di Milano. Laura Grassi is Resarch Vice Director of the Fintech & Insurtech Observatory. Nadir Snounois a Research Analyst at the Fintech & Insurtech Observatory.

makers in a financial service or segment, in that they have conquered only a modest market share. What is often significant to note, however, is the initial footprint left by these companies, indicating new directions, and opening frontiers, new ways of operating and distinguishing competencies that gradually show up in the organizational structures of the traditional stakeholders too, resulting in profound changes. This is borne out by the fact that startups working in areas that are not yet regulated get on average 205 per cent more funding; that startups that automate client management more assertively receive 192 per cent more funding; and that more and more Fintech startups are collaborating with traditional stakeholders. Against this backdrop, the Italian world of banking and finance, which has always remained on the side-lines of these phenomena, more concerned with fundamental structural matters, now seems to have woken up and is trying to catch up via various initiatives, the effects of which can already be seen, even in the short term.

Third, the emergence of ecosystems that offer an alternative to bank trust – one of the founding factors and the value proposition of the world of finance – with blockchain and bitcoin being the most relevant technical and market examples. In fact, bitcoin opened the door to new ways of managing trust in transactions, offering alternative systems to the traditional methods. Even if it is still too soon to define the limits of its application, it is evident that some environments have already shown clear potential and benefits from this and similar technologies and there is no doubt that it will leave a significant mark. The figures related to cryptocurrencies demonstrate how fluctuating the situation still is: in addition to bitcoin, which alone accounts for around 61 per cent of the overall monetary mass in cryptocurrencies, there are at least 898 other cryptocurrencies in the world, but, it is important to note, when taken all together, on a global scale they do not equal even 0.5 per cent of the monetary aggregate of bank notes, coins and financial activities that can be used as means of payment.

Historically, external pressures on the financial market have largely prevailed over internal ones to become drivers of change for financial institutions. Recently, however, we are witnessing the emergence of important change drivers coming from inside some banking and financial organizations too. Of these, we would like to highlight three in particular:

1) An increasing awareness of data management as a means of value creation. Banks and financial institutions are sitting on enormous deposits of data, of 'digital black gold' that should be located, extracted and refined by the appropriate organizations, able to express its value in every business process, especially the core processes, that is, risk assessment and management. Although the road is still long, awareness of this value is gaining strength and currency:

in the last year alone the Italian market for big data analytics for the banking sector grew by almost 30 per cent, the biggest growth of any sector even in terms of market share, which stands at 28 per cent, despite strong growth in sectors linked to Industry 4.0[2] which have benefited significantly from incentives. The world of insurance is still lagging behind, however.

2) Artificial intelligence is starting to become a tangible reality. The world of finance, which has historically made substantial use of automatic algorithms to manage some services such as payments or trading, is seeing the blossoming of initiatives that use artificial intelligence and machine learning in various ways. We surveyed more than 50 chatboxes used by financial institutions at international level (by no means exhaustive), and we analysed more than 110 forms of robo advisoring[3] at international level. Some of these experiments have already resulted in a marketable proposition, have paved the way and are gaining a lot of attention from many market stakeholders.
3) The emergence of new organizational structures that are more suited to finance with a digital DNA. Organizational models mutated from the agile and lean startup paradigms are becoming an increasingly frequent experiment for at least some sections of banking organizations, supported by digital instruments that help the bank working context better respond to the demands of a digital market in continuous and rapid evolution, and which have even made the bank work context more enjoyable. This can be seen in the fact that financial institutions start to stand out among the best places to work, in the by now noticeable presence of advanced client relationship models, such as bank spoke branches, better able to manage intrinsically digital omnichannel processes, and in the confirmed interest among top university students in the world of finance.

It is clear therefore that the context is still very fluid and not very consolidated, especially regarding the boundaries that can delimit the various stakeholders and the various market segments. In addition, there is a technological component, APIs (application programming interfaces) with strong organizational implications, fundamental for governing such fluid boundaries. The APIs allow for considerable increases in flexibility in terms of cost and time with which a banking or insurance institute can change its own sphere of activity, even in light of the advent of PSD2.

---

2 The Industry 4.0 is the cyber-physical transformation of productive systems and organization.

3 Robo-advisors are a class of financial advisers which provide financial advice or investment management online with minimal human intervention.

1. Innovation in retail banking and business model

From the survey conducted of over fifty banks and fifteen banking groups, aimed at monitoring the current situation in the Italian retail banking world and the relationship channels most used with clients, we can see the start of a transformation process in interactions with clients, although not always with clearly defined strategies.

A study of the physical network of branches and ATMs, which are the traditional points of contact with clients, shows how institutions are willing to rethink spaces and service modes for users, although frequently with different strategies.

Banking institutions are consolidating and are seeking to automate some operations to reduce the need to actively involve operators, which has led to a reduction in the number of bank branches in Italy, according to Banca d'Italia. In fact, the number of bank and post office counters shrank by 4 per cent over the course in 2017, from 43,160 to 41,600 with the drop almost entirely attributable to the banking sector (down from almost 30,300 to just over 29,000 branches). The survey conducted by the Observatory shows how the majority of branches are still traditional, that is, based on a counter that customers use for any type of operation. A minority of banks have installed self-service kiosks inside some branches (generally between 10 per cent and 20 per cent of the branch network), that allow clients to conduct some informative and deposit operations by themselves (including, for example, depositing cheques, paying F24 and MAV/RAV forms), thus reducing workload for the employees and reducing queueing times for clients.

Some institutions are pursuing the same objective but focusing on the functions of the ATMs located outside the banks. Our survey shows that practically all institutions have a totally multifunctional park of ATMs, and a large percentage of these are ATMs that also allow customers to make deposits in cash and/or cheque. More specifically, over 20 per cent of ATMs are 'advanced' and accept deposits, but here again we see differing strategies: some banks believe firmly in this tool, and around 50 per cent of their ATMs are of this type, while others have not pushed in this direction, and just over 10 per cent are of this type.

Only very few banks have decided to dedicate space inside their branches to allow clients to call an operator in a video call from a specially equipped station and to conduct transactions linked to shares or loans. Only two of the banks interviewed offered this possibility and a further two are testing it, but without much conviction.

Moving on to more digital channels of communication – PC, smartphone and tablet – we can see that these are becoming the carrier channels of banks' retail strategy. Data shows that on average 38 per cent of total bank clients are active online banking users via PC (up 5 per cent from last year), and in some institutions this is over 47 per cent of total clients. Each PC user executes an average of around 14 transactions per year, with some banks recording peaks of 30 transactions.

The mobile channel (smartphone and tablet) is currently slightly less commonplace, but with reasonable certainty we believe it will become the channel of choice for interaction with clients. On average, 15 per cent of clients of the banks interviewed are active smartphone or tablet users, up from the 9 per cent recorded by the same banks in 2015. Some institutions which have focused heavily on digital channels, introducing a multichannel relationship with their clients right from the outset, have already recorded peaks of 28 to 30 per cent of users active via mobile channels. Each active smartphone or tablet user conducts an average of six banking transactions per year, with peaks of nine transactions.

2. Fintech startups: driver of digital transformation?

Digital has revolutionized the financial sector, both in terms of actors involved and tools available to them. The offer of financial services is constantly expanding with new players coming in as suppliers to or competitors of the traditional financial institutions. Among these players, new companies play a fundamental role. Fintech startups launched in recent years with the aim of entering the financial market, positioning themselves as serious competitors (mostly in the initial phases of the phenomenon) or as suppliers to banks (a much more recent trend, especially in Italy and in the European Union).

Internationally we have surveyed 730 Fintech startups that received over 1 million dollars, for a total of almost $26 billion of financing from institutional investors, banks, large technology providers and business angels. In fact, there is no lack of partnerships between startups and traditional actors, with one startup in three having started at least one – a strategic collaboration that can allow a financial institution to innovate more quickly, testing new roads with more limited investments.

Figure 15: Distribution of startups by geographical area.

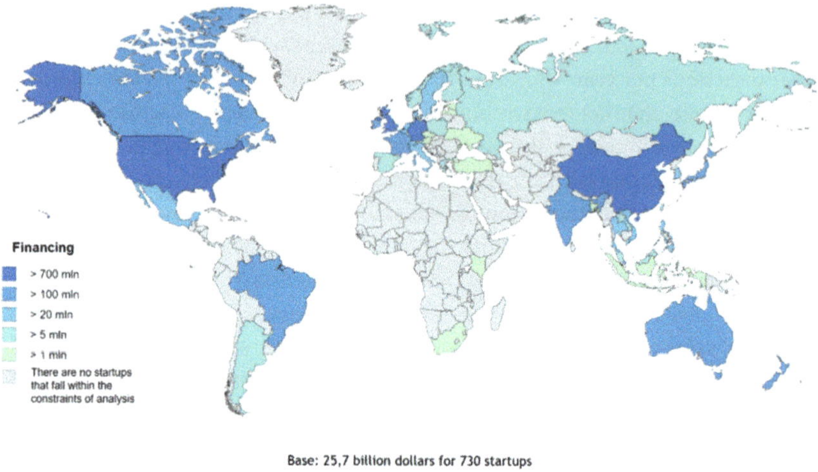

Specifically, most of the funding was raised in the US ($15.6 billion) and in China ($4 billion). On the European continent, the United Kingdom ($2 billion) and Germany ($0.7 billion) are the countries in which more funding has been collected (Figure 15).

Only 5 per cent of the analysed startups explicitly offer a service to banks, effectively establishing themselves as their supplier or collaborator.

The remaining 95 per cent of startups, on the other hand, are a concrete alternative to banks, divided almost equally between those that target the final consumer (B2C, identified with 'Consumer', 50 per cent of the sample, 70 per cent in terms of financing) and those that refer to a business target, such as SMEs and corporate companies (B2B, 35 per cent). However, it is important to underline how, among these, there are some startups that address at the same time more than one kind of non-bank actor.

The startups have the advantage of being able to exploit some differential levers such as the possibility of operating without the need to have a physical network in the territory and having the opportunity to exploit in a native way the large amount of data they collect, or to move with greater ease within the grey areas of regulation.

A dynamic energy movement with large resources available that makes available to the financial world significant solutions and proposals (in ideas, in people, in experimentation, in business models, and so on). For a financial institution, the management of the change brought about by digital cannot be separated from the monitoring and acquisition of value from the new actors and from the elaboration of a strategy to use the tools that digital makes available.

These new companies are of various different types (Figure 16) and include some who offer purely banking services (opening and managing an account, payments, loans and financing, and so on), others who propose investment solutions, insurance and, finally, some startups which while not strictly financial provide support services specifically for the finance sector (for example, marketing or big data management).

The largest category, 60 per cent of startups (and 73 per cent of financing), is banking services which includes services related to account management, payments and financing, followed by investment services (19 per cent of the total) which include services related to asset management and in general to capital markets. The other services category (16 per cent of startups) offers services that are not strictly financial but that address the financial world. Finally, a remaining 5 per cent of the total number of startups offers insurance services.

Figure 16: Distribution of the main types and financing.

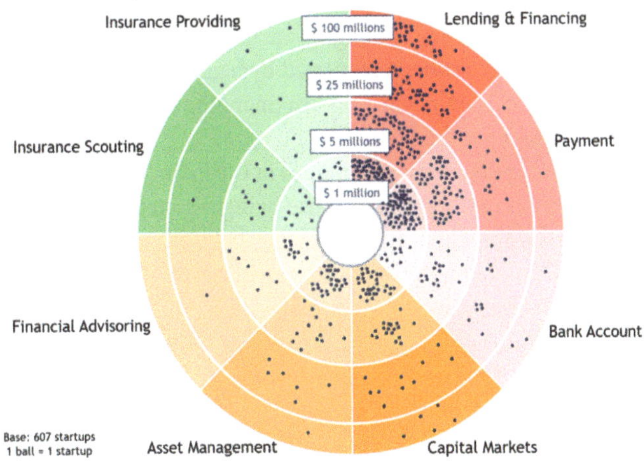

The relevance of the banking category (red zone in Figure 16) is almost entirely due to the lending and financing startups, which have met with great success, gathering 60 per cent of total financing (about $15 billion).

The category of payment services, however, compared to the high number of startups (34 per cent of the banking category) has collected a significantly lower percentage of financing (10 per cent of the banking category which corresponds to 7 per cent of the total).

Although almost one-fifth of startups focus on investment services (orange zone in Figure 16), this type of service only accounts for 9 per cent of funding, recording the lowest average funding.

Insurance startups (green zone in Figure 16) are those that overall receive the highest average financing with $61.5 million. Startups scouting insurance policies account for more than half of the total number of insurance startups, but receive only 9 per cent of funding.

About 90 per cent of startups in the 'other services' category is distributed almost equally between the security, accounting/HR and big data sectors.

Regardless of the type of service offered, the success of every initiative depends on various factors (financial, strategic, entrepreneurial, luck, and so on). We have identified some factors linked to the business model that many startups which have received funding have in common, and that we therefore believe can increase the chances of success of the solutions developed (see Figure 17). In the specific case of Fintech startups we have identified the following attributes that also show real behaviours observed in the new companies and that attract higher than average capital investment:

1) The intention to take advantage of grey areas in regulations, that is, operating in areas that have not yet been regulated by legislators. Startups which operate in this area have been rewarded with financing of on average 205 per cent higher than average for the sector.
2) The mass use of big data. New companies in the financial market which create their own key assets with the careful use of big data receive an average of 192 per cent more funding than the mean.
3) Developing special digital channels to provide their service. Fintech startups that develop their own business model focusing on an intensive and efficient use of digital channels receive on average 85 per cent more than the average for the sector.

Figure 17: Difference in funding according to the individual success factors.

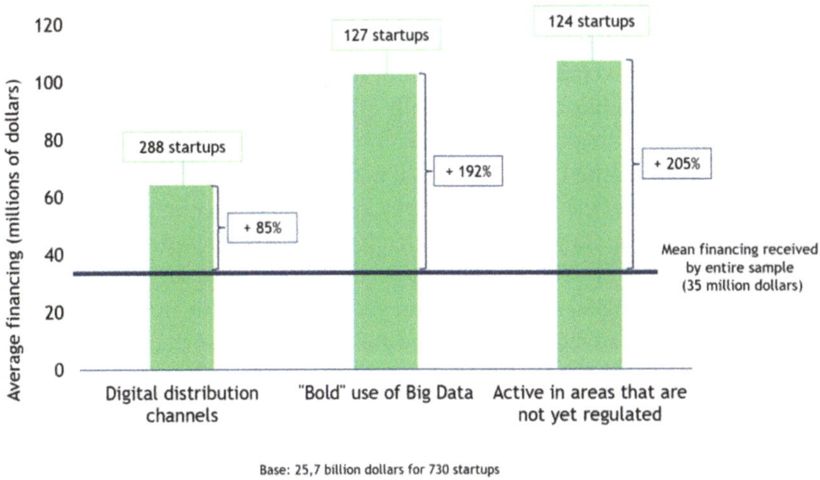

The importance of these factors is even more striking if taken all together: the more key success factors the startups use, the more the average financing grows. Startups that do not present any of these three success variables receive 56 per cent less financing than average, while those that blend all three success factors are rewarded with an average financing that is 482 per cent more than the average for the sector.

It is evident therefore that traditional companies must also monitor these factors closely, even if it is just to monitor the traces that this strong investment will leave on the market, regardless of whether or not the startup is successful.

3. Big Techs are moving... but in what direction?

Diverse players, not purely financial (we surveyed 51 at international level) are increasingly expanding their own initiatives into financial activity segments, offering one or more proprietary solutions (we polled 123, with a total of 157 financial services), developed in-house (60 per cent of the solutions) or in collaboration with traditional financial players such as banks and insurance companies (24 per cent of solutions) or with other types of stakeholders (non-financial companies, Fintech startups, service providers, 16 per cent).

Forty businesses which offer financial services, accounting for 78 per cent of the sample, are stakeholders that we believe pose the biggest threat to the incumbents of the financial world. They are particularly diversified and include large corporations (50 per cent), digital stakeholders (22 per cent), technology providers (10 per cent) and telecommunication companies (18 per cent).

The large corporations are mainly subdivided between retail (55 per cent) and automotive (40 per cent). Sixty per cent of these stakeholders have their main base in Europe and most operate globally (70 per cent). Specifically, five retail stakeholders have already launched their own online and in-store banks. The companies based in the USA such as Walmart, ASDA (operating in the United Kingdom, but part of the Walmart group), Costco and Kroger on the other hand offer various solutions in partnership with other players, taking advantage of their physical and digital presence to offer financial and diversified services.

Turning to the digital stakeholders, we see that they mostly operate at global level (89 per cent of all digital players) and are of American (56 per cent) or Asian (44 per cent) origin. They include ICT service providers (70 per cent) which mainly offer digital payment solutions, such as Facebook, Google or Microsoft, and pure e-commerce players (30 per cent) which offer additional types of financial service (for example, Alibaba offers wealth management, financial consulting and credit rating services). There are four technology providers and they offer digital payment solutions with digital wallets that are accessible from smartphones or from smart watches or other devices. This category includes solutions offered by companies such as Apple and Samsung. The telecommunications companies, finally, mostly offer digital payment solutions, but then there are cases like Orange, for example, who have launched an online and mobile bank in both France and Poland.

As in Figure 18, 5 per cent of the financial solutions mapped are Complement (see the notes on methodology, below), correlated to the core business of the non-financial company and mostly aimed at existing clients while 8 per cent of cases are Concentric, correlated to the core business but aimed at both existing and new clients. Thirty-one per cent are Horizontal, that is, not directly correlated to the core business of the non-financial company and are aimed solely at existing clients, while the remaining 56 per cent of cases are Conglomerate, that is, solutions dedicated to both new and existing clients and not correlated to the core business of the company.

In total, 64 per cent of the solutions are offered to new clients, highlighting the fact that most players tend to offer solutions to break into the financial sector, and not with the sole objective of expanding and strengthening their own offering of products and services.

Figure 18: Strategic positioning of the financial services offered by non-financial companies.

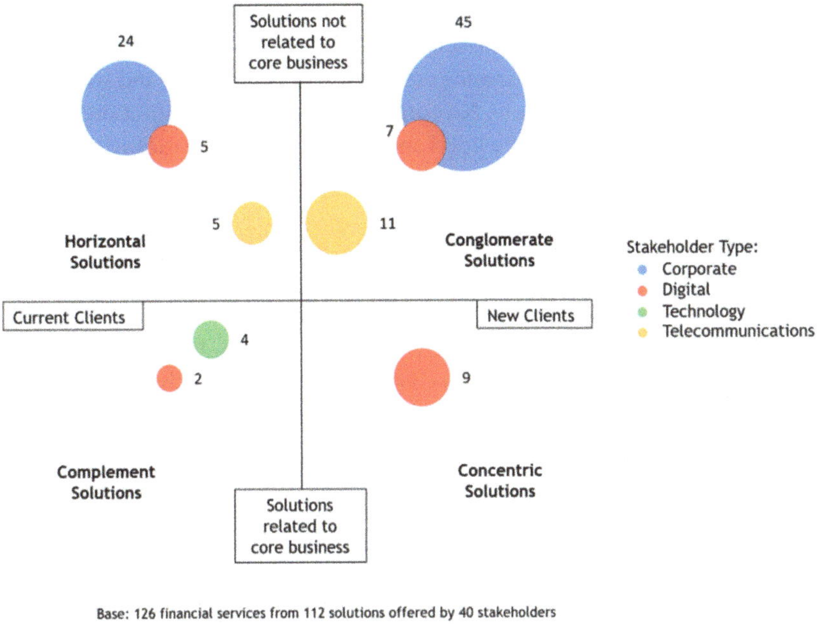

Appendix

Research methodology: The results presented were attained using various research methods, as described below.

Literature review: We analysed hundreds of indirect sources that we deemed most relevant for each strand of research. The sources used were mostly academic articles, professional reports, strategic plans and other documents issued directly by financial institutions. We also analysed the main national and international news reports related to each area of analysis.

Quantification of innovative retail banking channels: In order to outline the impact of digital innovation on the evolution of retail banking channels, we distributed a survey to over 50 Italian banks and fifteen banking groups, representing over 90 per cent of the Italian market and aimed at monitoring the current situation of Italian retail banking, and at monitoring which communication channels are used most frequently to communicate with clients.

The analysis looked closely at the key aspects regarding the type of communication channel between the financial institution and their clients: branches, self-service stations and video calls in branches with consultants; advanced ATMs; PCs; mobile, comprising smartphone and tablet. We also analysed other innovative services, such as robo advisors.

Census of Fintech startups: The census, conducted in December 2016, looked at all startups in the area of Finance that were set up after 2011 and which had received funding between 1 June 2014 and 31 May 2016 from institutional investors, banks, large technology providers and business angels. We excluded startups that by the end of May 2016 had received less than $1 million in total funding. The total number of startups in our poll was around 730 who had received a total of almost $26 billion in funding.

We also monitored new startups financed during 2017 via secondary sources.

Analysis of extended competition: This analysis concentrated on financial services offered by non-financial international companies or by financial companies belonging to a non-financial company (for example, a retailer), selecting only large stakeholders (classification based on size according to European Commission Recommendation 2003/361/EC).

The sample selected in this way consists of 60 international businesses that provide a total of 122 solutions that can be classified as banking, insurance or other financial services. The data was collected from analysis of the companies' websites, and from articles published in specialist and generalist press. The sources consulted include reports (for example, from leading consulting companies), international press (for example, Fintech and financial services newsletters, the *Financial Times*) and sector-specific press (for example, Finextra, Fintech Weekly).

The survey looked only at the solutions offered.

We excluded financial solutions such as credit cards that can only be used in one specific company, fuel cards or finance for purchasing specific products and payment in instalments.

Francesca Rosati and Teresa Spada[1]

Focus 2: Established Banks and Tech Giants – Friends or Competitors?

ABI Lab through the Observatory on Fintech Innovation, which includes 14 banking groups, investigates several topics. Among them, it researches the impacts of GAFA on the business models of established financial actors. In particular, it studies the possible factors which may explain the perceived large gap in innovation between incumbents, Fintechs and Big Techs.

As Figure 19 shows, incumbents' representatives acknowledge that Fintechs and Big Techs have a competitive advantage in both the time required to launch new digital services on the market and the capability to collect and analyse data. Therefore, incumbents should improve their 'time to market' in order to not lose competitiveness against new actors entering the financial ecosystem.

Figure 19: Perceived gaps with Fintechs and Big Techs.

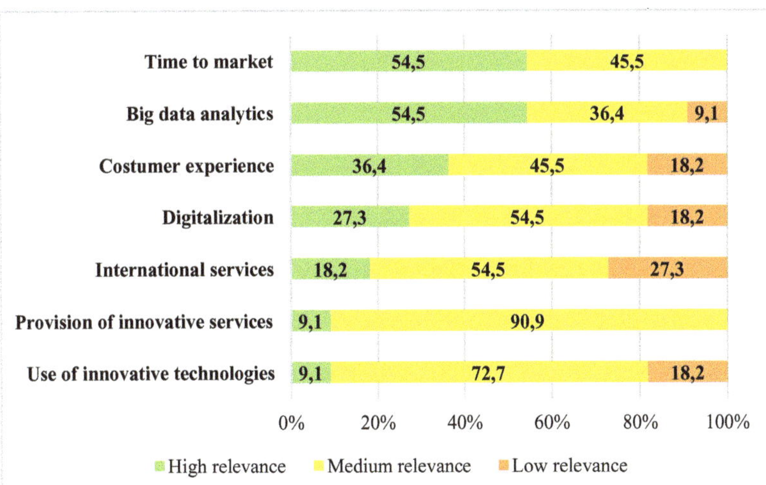

Source: Authors' elaboration from ABI Lab, Fintech Innovation Observatory, November 2018; 11 banks – which represent 54 per cent of the Italian banking industry by total assets – were interviewed.

1 Francesca Rosati is Senior Research Analyst at ABI Lab. Teresa Spada is Institutional Project Manager at ABI Lab.

The ABI Lab survey also shows that the competitive push in the financial sector will prevail over payment services followed by the credit sector and finally over digital cards.

Instead, there is a competitive minors pressure on digital banking, wealthtech and crowfunding platforms.

Regarding data, it must be underlined that even though Big Techs collect a huge amount of data on consumer behaviours, banks possess information about their customers that is high quality and could potentially be used more efficiently.

In a context where consumer data represent a key element of competition, there should be greater attention paid to the new concept of the open data economy. This consists of the idea that the real owner of data is the final consumer, who can decide to share them with market operators. Therefore, clients should be given the means to manage their own data. It should be permissible to share data with banks also, even when collected by GAFA, on factors such as preferences, behaviours and purchases.

Among the assets that banks consider the most important factors for their competitiveness, aside from data, are their historic competence in financial services and their trust relationship with clients. In fact, banks, in addition to establishing a personal relationship with their clients thanks to their physical branches, ensure high security standards for their digital services.

Cristiana Schena and Alessandra Tanda[1]

Focus 3: The Development of Digital Strategy and Business Models in Banking Activities

The rapid changes generated by digital economy developments are impacting all business activities (OECD 2017) and determining especially intense effects on the financial sector. The principal international banks have launched digital development plans (Tanda 2018) partly in an attempt to make their production and distribution processes more efficient and reduce costs for the purposes of profitability, put considerably to the test in the decade which began with the 2008 crisis. This redefinition of banking strategic plans and business models was also triggered by competitive pressures taking practical shape within the banking sector whose confines are progressively widening to encompass new digital native finance firms.

This is especially a question of Fintech firms set up with the primary objective of offering financial services exclusively and Techfin, which were pre-existing technology and e-commerce firms which moved into the financial services sector subsequently (Zetzsche 2017, Schena et al. 2018: 24). The so-called Big Tech companies[2] also fall within Techfin as their diversification strategies from original core business included developing financial activities. The financial resources, level of technological development and information acquired over time on the wide customer base at Big Techs' disposal have led to these being defined 'digital disruptors' (WEF and Deloitte 2017).[3] In fact they use especially advanced technological solutions which enable them to intercept financial needs and acquire

1 Cristiana Schena is Full Professor in Economics of Financial Intermediaries at the University of Insubria. Alessandra Tanda is Researcher in Economics of Financial Intermediaries at the University of Pavia.

2 The main Big Tech firms include US Google, Apple, Amazon, Facebook (GAFA), Chinese Baidu, Alibaba and Tencent (BAT) and Japanese Sony and AEON.

3 See also 'Big Tech in AI: What Amazon, Apple, Google, GE, and Others are Working On', in *CB Insights*, 12 October 2017, https://www.cbinsights.com/research/top-tech-companies-artificial-intelligence-expert-intelligence; 'Banks On Notice: Fintechs are Coming for Checking Accounts & Debit Cards', in *CB Insights*, 2 August 2018, https://www.cbinsights.com/research/fintech-checking-accounts-debit-card-disruption.

and process large volumes of information relating to customers;[4] as technologies progressively enable soft information to be replaced by big-data analysis, competition with banks will grow further, competition which is already intense in payments, standardized consumer credit, brokerage of securities and passively managed funds spheres (Gobbi 2016).

In accordance with the wishes of the Financial Stability Board (2017) and employing a proprietary database, this focus analyses the specific features and advantages of the strategic approaches adopted by Big Techs (section 1 below) to compare these with those offered by the main international banks (section 2 below). On the basis of case studies, this study contributes to the next generation of banking business model debate which, in theoretical terms, was effectively summarized in the recent BIS-BCBS report (Basel Committee on Banking Supervision 2018). The concluding section of this contribution will briefly consider the results of our analysis which offer insights into forecast evolutions in the banking and financial sectors (paragraph 3).

1. Big Tech strategies in the financial services sector

In line with the Fintech sector, Big Tech firms offer innovative financial services via digital applications or platforms (open API, electronic platforms or digital marketplaces) which facilitate client contact and enable customer needs to be fulfilled rapidly thanks to immediate service access.

In this way the approach traditionally adopted by incumbent banks via physical proximity to clients is replaced with 'digital proximity' which takes the form of financial services usable beyond any geographical borders separating financial body and customer. This gives an insight into the dynamics which Fintech developments are generating in customer mind-set changes with customers appreciating the ability of these firms to offer easy to access solutions satisfying their financial demands in short time frames. This also explains the progressive growth in client faith in Fintech, especially amongst the young and digitalized (Capgemini et al. 2017), as well as the powerful reputation which has been making Big Tech attractive to many consumers for years now (Barba Navaretti et al. 2017, IOSCO 2017), including in competition with dominant sector firms (Baker et al. 2017).

---

4 Effectively the Big Tech firms acquire data relating to their habits and spending preferences and purchase payment methods free of charge from users on their platforms and Internet sites: this volume of data feeds the algorithms which elaborate information automatically which is used to offer these same users services of various kinds, including financial services.

Thus speed, attention to customers and flexibility are key elements in the eyes of clients choosing financial services (EBA 2018).

These competitive advantages are especially intense for Big Techs, given their ability to personalise their services, thus raising customer-experience levels.[5] Big Techs are effectively interested not only in the shopping by its clients on its digital platforms or apps, but also, and primarily, in a relationship based on 'customer care and support' as well as interaction with the brand. In other words, clients must have all their needs satisfied thanks to a single interlocutor who knows how to simplify access to services and even forecast client needs and anticipate their responses. Big Tech thus has a strong competitive advantage greater than Fintech's and much feared by dominant sector firms too (incumbent banks).

A further element of special relevance in highlighting the specific features of the new financial operators is the way the processes underlying financial services provision is managed as these have been revealed to be deeply different from those adopted by the banks. As is well known, in order to satisfy clients' multiplicity of financial requirements in an integrated way, banks adopt a 'universal' or multi-business model which is developed by creating complex group structures. This approach exposes them to the risks linked to financial services offered to customers and subjects them to much more restrictive and burdensome regulations than those to which Fintech companies are subject. These latter, by contrast, adopt a very different operational approach based on the 'unbundling'[6] of financial services. This generates a breakup of production processes determining 'specialist' service provision by means of the creation of direct financial circuits (digital platforms) or other technological solutions (such as apps). On the one hand this approach enables clients to complete their financial transactions directly and without using intermediaries and regulated financial markets. On the other hand it enables Fintech firms to avoid exposing themselves to the financial risks inherent in the services they offer their customers and, also, to exploit operational spaces not specifically subject to regulatory controls. For this reason, for some time now, it has been argued that Fintech is capable of generating 'banking without the bank'

5 Customer experience can be defined as the whole of consumer experiences in their interaction with the firm from whom they buy products and services.

6 Unbundling is a method involving breaking down products and services into parts so that only parts of it can be provided according to need. For example, unbundling makes it possible to provide a limited scope of services, such as payments and loans, instead of providing all banking services including payments, deposits, loans, and asset management all together.

(Worthington and Welch 2011) and replacing established banking firms in spheres in which its services coincide.

To further elaborate these considerations, we believe that it is appropriate to consider the strategic choices made by the financially most active players. Our analysis will focus on six Big Tech firms for which it has been possible to source mutually comparable information: the US GAFA and Chinese Tencent and Alibaba.

A first interesting element which emerges relates to the wide range of financial services offered by Big Tech companies ranging from payment services to lending and asset management. Furthermore, thanks to the use of digital distribution channels, these services are offered in geographical areas differing from those in which Big Tech firms developed their original non-financial activities. It is also clear that, while Fintech users are primarily retail (Schena et al. 2018), Big Tech firms' core business has generated customers which also encompasses the firms they work with or which offer goods and services through their platforms.

Our analysis has revealed that financial services provision is, in most cases, the outcome of in-house strategic development. The services and products designed by Big Tech firms are then offered and distributed via subsidiary and associate firms. If requested by the legislation of those countries in which they work, these group companies are authorized to work as regulated financial intermediaries. Moreover, in many cases, financial services provision also takes place on the basis of partnership agreements.

A more in-depth look at the specific features of the individual cases examined brings out two different strategic approaches currently being used by Big Tech firms to develop their financial services. The first is essentially a matter of offering financial services instrumental to reinforcing their core business. This strategic approach has been used right through to today by US Big Tech firms (Google, Apple, Facebook, Amazon). The second targets a strong diversification objective which takes shape via the creation of complex and variously structured conglomerates. This has been the strategy of Chinese Big Tech firms Tencent and Alibaba.

Specifically, Apple, Facebook and Google have developed in-house payment systems to work in the domestic market, activating money transmitter or payment institute licences. Furthermore, on their foreign markets Apple and Google offer payment services in partnership with banks, consumer credit institutions and existing payment circuits.

Amazon first developed payment systems to favour rapid and simple purchase payments on its site. Subsequently it offered lending services for both consumers (via traditional or revolving credit cards) and the small businesses which sell their products via the Amazon site.

Note that the unbundling of financial services enables Big Tech and the majority of Fintech firms to develop this type of strategic approach without requiring a banking licence and, frequently (depending on the legal standards in the countries they work in), without being subject to controls on the financial activities undertaken. At the same time, through the rebundling of the services offered by a multiplicity of firms and financial operators, Big Tech firms have succeeded in selecting and combining solely the services required by their customers and offering these as 'new' financial products.[7] Customers thus perceive Big Tech firms as capable of satisfying all their needs, including on the financial level. The legal solution adopted by these Big Tech firms is radically different from that traditionally implemented by incumbent banking groups. For example, Amazon primarily makes use of partnerships rather than acquisitions for the development of its financial services in its main reference markets (the USA and India).

With reference to the second strategic approach, adopted by Tencent and Alibaba, it can be highlighted that these two Big Techs have pursued intense diversification strategies even by setting up a bank and a financial group within their industrial groups.

In particular, Tencent (whose core business is made up principally of entertainment services, mass media, Internet and communication) has been developing payment apps for years and set up WeBank in 2015, one of the first authorized online banks in China. WeBank principally offers the products of other financial intermediaries and itself grants consumer loans for small sums via its Weilidai platform. The bank has many partnerships with a range of Chinese financial intermediaries including banks, insurance firms and asset management companies. These agreements enable WeBank to distribute its partner banks' products, too. Additionally, Tencent has developed further Fintech services (including wallets, consumer credit and payments services) and manages an asset management platform (LiCaiTong). In October 2017 Tencent also obtained a licence for the distribution of insurance products and began activating partnerships in this area of financial activity.

The other Chinese Big Tech firm, Alibaba (whose core business is made up principally of e-commerce services), entered the financial sector in 2004 when it set up Fintech Alipay specialising in payments. Alipay's service provision was initially via partnerships with certain Chinese banks. It later obtained a payment business licence from the People's Bank of China and a third-party payment

7 Rebundling is a method involving unbundling financial products provided by different companies, and selecting and combining only the services consumers need, offering them as a new financial product.

platform for fund transactions licence from the China Securities Regulatory Commission. Since 2013, thanks to its partnership with Chinese firm Tianhong Asset Management, Alipay has enabled its customers to invest in Yu'e Bao investment funds, born as Alipay client support services. This fund enables clients to set aside residual sums when making payments through the app using their smartphones.

In 2014 Alibaba set up Ant Financial Services Group which originated with Alipay. Ant Financial obtained a banking licence in China and leads the Alibaba group's financial sub-holding company. In the context of this sub-holding group, Ant Financial set up MYbank in 2014, which obtained a Chinese market banking licence; MYbank operates online only. Ant Financial offers lending, cash management and insurance services in the domestic market as well as payment services for Chinese customers the world over. In May 2018 Ant Financial included a further two funds in its service range, managed by asset management partners (Bosera Asset Management Co., Ltd and Zhong Ou Asset Management Co., Ltd) in which all the Alibaba group's customers can invest.

2. Digitalization development in the large international banks

The European Banking Authority analysis has detected two main trends ('digital transformation' and 'digital disruption') in the multiplicity of strategic approaches adopted by banks in the new digitalization context (EBA 2018). The EBA report underlines that these two principal strategic choices involve different levels of organizational and business model change. In fact, in the case of digital transformation, banks implement generally in-house strategies based on the creation of digital channels aimed essentially at digitalising and optimising procedures, reducing costs and improving efficiency. Adopting a digital disruption approach is more pervasive and its ultimate goal is to seek out new revenues and satisfy new client demands.

To acquire additional evaluation elements on the future business model scenarios in the banking activity context, we have deepened the results that emerged from previous studies on the subject of the strategic choices taken in individual firms (Tanda 2018). For this purpose we used a proprietary database regarding 32 incumbent firms who have been especially active in the digitalization process[8] on

8 The banks included in the sample are: ABN Amro, BBVA, Banco do Brasil, Bank of China, BNY Mellon, Barclays, BNP Paribas, Citigroup, Commerzbank, Credit Agricole, Credit Mutuel, Credit Suisse, Deutsche Bank, DZ Bank, Goldman Sachs, Groupe BPCE, HSBC, ING, Intesa Sanpaolo, JP Morgan Chase, Lloyds Banking Group, Morgan

which we have found homogeneous and significant information for our analysis.[9] This will enable the understanding of the intensity of change which the main international banks are undergoing to compete with Big Tech firms.

First and foremost, what emerges is that the sample's banks have activated a multiplicity of initiatives in different financial intermediation areas (loans, personal finance, trading platforms, wealth management, payments, insurance services) and in technological activities functional or instrumental to financial activities (blockchain, data analytics, security, compliance and data protection systems, regtech). Moreover, there is no area in which a single strategic approach is used.

Considering the degree of intensity of the initiatives, it is clear that the banks have paid particular attention to digital developments in payment services which constitute the original field developed by Fintech and fully developed by Big Tech. In this area the banks have adopted a range of strategic approaches, sometimes simultaneously. In particular, seventeen banks have acquired shares in Fintech, eight have signed partnership agreements and eleven have developed in-house projects.

The interest by incumbent firms in blockchain-type technologies is also extremely high. In this field twenty-three banks have invested in tech companies and only one has activated a partnership with a tech firm.

In-house development has been chosen by the majority of banks in the fields of personal finance and online banking activities (devoted, principally, to retail clients), wealth management, security, compliance and data protection. It probably depends on the will of the large banks to proceed to internal development of the main core business areas and those producing the greatest added value as well as activities linked to the internal controls system which are of strategic importance for customer relations development, too.

By contrast, as regards the development of other financial services and instrumental tools, the strategic approach most intensively adopted has been acquiring Fintech and tech shares. This is presumably a consequence of the will of the banks to identify rapid solutions for the development of specific operational contexts in which Fintech and tech firms have now acquired considerable expertise and developed effective technological solutions.

Using the classification identified by EBA mentioned above, we can also highlight that the majority of banks in our sample are undergoing a digital

---

Stanley, MUFG-Bank of Tokyo, Natixis, Nordea Bank, Rabobank, Royal Bank of Scotland, Santander, Société Générale, Standard Chartered, UBS, Unicredit.

9 This information was drawn from the firms' Internet sites, balance sheets and financial reports, shareholder presentations and road shows, press releases and industrial plans where these are publicly available.

transformation process. This process is based essentially on development and diversification of the distributional channels for the purposes of attracting new customer segments (and millennials in the first place), maintaining market shares or, at least, limiting losses of customers to Fintech and Big Tech platforms, reducing costs and making the distribution process more efficient.

Only in a few cases the strategic planning appears more advanced and based on innovation not only of distributional aspects but also in production processes (digital disruption). Moreover, it not a foregone conclusion that this latter approach will spread; this is because of the organizational difficulties which incumbent firms may encounter in implementing these strategies, above all traceable to legacy issues and the impact on human resources and operational methods. The slow pace of implementation in change trajectories also emerges. We believe that this is due to the complexity of the reconversion processes operating within banks and, to an even greater extent, a complex group structure. The effective degree of digitalization pursued by the individual banks in the sample varies widely.

3. A few considerations on the future of the financial system

This focus has enabled us to highlight significant differences between the strategic approaches adopted by Big Techs and the principal international banks they compete with to all intents and purposes on the development of digitalization in financial services in the context of the new digital economy.

In particular, the unbundling and rebundling of the productive processes, IT processing methods and innovation in the approach to clients highlight a deep change which the banking activities developed by Big Tech are undergoing, above all in reference to the retail customer segment (individuals and small and medium-sized enterprises).

In various ways the competitive threat exerted by Fintech to the traditional financial system is a credible and pervasive one. This is even more true of Big Tech, which enjoys a large information database, consolidated relationships of trust with its customer base, very advanced technology and huge financial resources to use to further expand its activities, including in the financial field.

To the disadvantage of the incumbents, then, scalability problems linked to the scale of technological investment and the potential to attract talent are generated, constituting crucial factors in the development and efficiency-generation in financial services. The main international banks are fully aware of the need to adopt a proactive strategic approach to grasp the opportunities offered by technological evolution, implement solutions coherent with the needs expressed by clients and respond effectively to the challenges inherent in new market scenarios.

Our analysis has also highlighted certain difficulties which impact on the speed and intensity of the development and reconversion processes generated within banking groups.

To this should be added that the competitive pressures may evolve further and rapidly, impacting progressively larger customer segments. The majority of financial activities are, in fact, easy to reproduce digitally, especially on the basis of an unbundling process which breaks down the value chain of traditional financial intermediation and allows new operators to exploit the most profitable phases in financial terms or the least onerous ones in terms of exposure to risk and legal compliance issues.

References

Baker, H. Kent, Greg Filbeck, Victor Ricciardi, eds (2017), *Financial Behavior: Players, Services, Products, and Markets*, Oxford, Oxford University Press.

Barba Navaretti, Giorgio, Giacomo Calzolari and Alberto Franco Pozzolo (2017), 'Fintech and Banks. Friends or Foes?', in *European Economy*, No. 2017.2 (December), https://european-economy.eu/?p=1954.

Basel Committee on Banking Supervision (2018), *Sound Practices. Implications of Fintech Developments for Banks and Bank Supervisors*, February, https://www.bis.org/bcbs/publ/d431.htm.

Capgemini, LinkedIn and Efma (2017), *World Fintech Report 2017*, https://www.capgemini.com/?p=84423.

EBA–European Banking Authority (2018), *EBA Report on the Impact of Fintech on Incumbent Credit Institutions' Business Models*, 3 July, https://eba.europa.eu/-/eba-assesses-risks-and-opportunities-from-fintech-and-its-impact-on-incumbents-business-models.

Financial Stability Board (2017), *Financial Stability Implications from Fintech. Supervisory and Regulatory Issues that Merit Authorities' Attention*, 27 June, http://www.fsb.org/?p=12911.

Gobbi, Giorgio (2016), *The Troubled Life of the Banking Industry*, Paper presented at the European Association of University Teachers of Banking and Finance Wolpertinger Conference 2016, Verona, 2 September, https://www.bancaditalia.it/pubblicazioni/interventi-vari/int-var-2016/Gobbi_02092016.pdf.

IOSCO–International Organization of Securities Commissions (2017), *IOSCO Research Report on Financial Technologies (Fintech)*, February, https://www.iosco.org/library/pubdocs/pdf/IOSCOPD554.pdf.

OECD (2017), *Key Issues for Digital Transformation in the G20*, Report prepared for a joint G20 German Presidency/OECD conference, Berlin, 12 January, https://www.oecd.org/g20/key-issues-for-digital-transformation-in-the-g20.pdf.

Tanda, Alessandra (2018), "The Digitalization of Foreign Banks", in Carlo Arlotta, Alessandra Piro and Andrea Uselli, eds, *Foreign Banks and Financial Intermediaries in Italy. The Support to Italian Economy in 2017*, AIBE–Associazione Italiana Banche Estere, June, https://www.aibe.it/?p=2090.

WEF–World Economic Forum and Deloitte (2017), *Beyond Fintech: A Pragmatic Assessment of Disruptive Potential in Financial Services*, August, https://www.weforum.org/reports/beyond-fintech-a-pragmatic-assessment-of-disruptive-potential-in-financial-services.

Worthington, Steve and Peter Welch (2011), "Banking Without the Banks", in *International Journal of Bank Marketing*, Vol. 29, No. 2, p. 190–201.

Zetzsche, Dirk et al. (2017), 'From FinTech to TechFin: The Regulatory Challenges of Data-Driven Finance', in *EBI Working Paper Series*, No. 6 (April), https://dx.doi.org/10.2139/ssrn.2959925; Schena, Cristiana et al. (2018), 'Lo sviluppo del Fintech. Opportunità e rischi per l'industria finanziaria nell'era digitale', in *Quaderni FinTech*, No. 1 (March), http://www.consob.it/web/area-pubblica/ft1.

Mariateresa Maggiolino[1]

Focus 4: Big Data Companies in Banking and Financial Services Markets: An Antitrust Issue?

1. Big data companies in the banking and financial services markets

So far, no institution or scholar has coined the conclusive notion of big data companies (hereinafter, BDCs). Nonetheless, the antitrust analysis of the big data phenomenon (Maggiolino 2018) makes it reasonable to use such an expression to identify the companies that, while offering their products and services, collect, even in real time, huge and diversified amounts of data, whether personal or not.

More precisely, since it is connected to the mere holding of big data, the notion of BDCs includes at least two kinds of firm. Firstly, it refers to companies that produce 'smart' objects through which the very same companies become recipients of constant data flows regarding the activities that individuals do with, or nearby the sensors of, those smart objects. Secondly, the notion of BDCs captures the actions of digital platforms that, by grouping together different categories of economic agents, with the ultimate goal of exploiting their interdependence,[2] gather data while engaging in two different activities: either they facilitate the meeting between sellers and buyers, as happens in the case of e-Bay and Amazon,[3] or they attract consumers' attention via zero-price services to offer advertisers, as happens in the case of Google and Facebook.[4]

Now, the availability of these data allows BDCs to analyse them in order to refine their offer, by increasingly enriching and differentiating it. This is the reason

---

1 Mariateresa Maggiolino is Associate Professor in Trade Laws, Bocconi University.

2 This is the case of indirect network effects. A firm enjoys direct network effects when its users' utility increases the more users join the network. Differently, a firm enjoys indirect network effects when it groups two demands, users and advertisers for example, and the more users join the firm, the higher advertisers' utility is. Under these circumstances, a firm is a platform.

3 In this case, we are talking about transaction platforms because between the categories of users who meet through the platform, trading activities are consumed.

4 In this other case, we talk about media platforms, because here the advertisers' category uses the platform to attract the attention of those users who use it, without consuming any direct transaction between them.

why BDCs are able to both operate in the most disparate markets and to enter easily markets of and in which they initially did not have any knowledge or expertise. In this regard, what is happening in the markets for banking and financial services is paradigmatic. Indeed, first, banking and financial services are awash with data. Second, the wide availability of data about variables such as payment habits, budget constraints or user solvency together with the use of big data analytics to profile customers and identify patterns of consumption allow BDCs to offer personalized products and services, or supporting finance and risk-control activities (Joint Committee of the European Supervisory Authorities 2016: 8–10), even without any previous expertise on the matter.

Not surprisingly, then, many BDCs are currently very active in the market for digital payment services, which indeed are constantly growing and are experiencing a form of significant renewal and technological change, with a simultaneous reduction in the costs of transfers, especially cross-border (Bansal et al. 2015). Thus, over the last five years, BDCs have developed software, such as Google Pay, Apple Pay or Amazon Pay, to make online and in-store digital payments, for the sake of users' ease. Indeed, these applications allow consumers to pay online and offline, by performing once only two single, simple and free operations: (i) provide the data necessary to create an account on the chosen application and (ii) associate to this account a credit or a prepaid card, on which the price to be paid will be charged. More recently, BDCs have been developing even simpler technologies that integrate the 'pay' function directly into an already widespread application, so that the customer, who is a user of these BDCs and who is interested in sending money to one or more individuals, will not even have to download new software to perform their transfers, both within a commercial relationship or as a donation. Instead, this user will access a messaging application, such as Facebook Messenger (Kottasova 2017), and simply click on the payment icon, provided that this function is also associated with a credit card or a prepaid card.

Certainly at present, it does not seem possible to return a comprehensive and definitive description of how the BDCs have chosen to configure their banking and financial services offerings.[5] The phenomenon, in fact, is not only very recent, but also very dynamic, given the 'ease' with which, adding a few lines of code to their platforms and forming a certain knowledge of the user, these companies can conceive and propose different and personalized offers that meet consumer

5 The European Banking Authority in Spring 2017 undertook a mapping exercise in order to gain a better insight into the financial services provided by Tech Firms and the technologies applied. See EBA (2017: 15–34).

preferences (Joint Committee of the European Supervisory Authorities 2016: 8–10).[6] However, the time is now ripe to dwell on why the BDCs follow the aforementioned strategies for expanding and differentiating their range of products and services, before discussing the antitrust profiles of this phenomenon.

2. Why big data companies enter new markets, such as those for banking and financial services

Prima facie, one might think that the motivation for the entrance of BDCs into new markets is their willingness to challenge companies that traditionally operate there, by leveraging the competitive advantage that they derive from digital technologies and digital data. However, more and more widespread in the literature is the idea that these BDCs are not really interested in pursuing this goal (Petit 2016). In other words, it is not believed that any new banking or financial service is designed to challenge banks, financial or payment institutions, but the justifications for these types of behaviour are different.

First of all, platforms innovate by developing new products and services, that is, they enter new markets, to enrich and expand the experience of their users and thus induce them to turn always to the same platform to meet all their needs – according to the so-called 'one-stop-shop theory'. In other words, each platform would cultivate a totalitarian aspiration: to 'suffice' for each user, by affirming its own ecosystem to the detriment of the rival's ecosystem. Secondly, platforms are not wishing to give any competitors the opportunity to experiment 'in solitary' in a potentially disruptive technological way. In other words, platforms are chasing each other in different secondary markets – that is, in markets other than their core business – to exclude the possibility that the one among them left free to experiment a new technological path in one of these secondary markets will find such an explosive innovation as to overwhelm all the other rival platforms, which instead would remain displaced and obsolete. Thirdly, and beyond these explanations that recall the idea of a competition that is not consumed in single sectors, but rather 'across industries', it is claimed that the platforms differentiate the range of services they offer to always access different data and, in this way, enrich and change the sources of information about their users.

6 The paper argues that the customization of the offered products and services will prevent offer standardization to the detriment of consumers' ability to compare the many alternative offers available.

3. Antitrust law and the entrance of big data companies in banking and financial markets

Antitrust law is not meant to protect consumers or competitors. It protects market well-functioning as it results from consumer welfare variations. In other words, business practices are anti-competitive when they limit output and increase market price, in the short run, or decrease quality, variety or innovation in the long run.

In general terms, antitrust law welcomes the entry of new companies into the market, not only because new entrants exert additional competitive pressures on incumbents, but also because new entrants often bring about innovations. Therefore, as a preliminary step, the entry of BDCs into the banking and financial services markets should not raise concerns in the antitrust authorities, which would probably see an increase in consumer welfare due to: (i) reduced consumer prices – financial and banking services are offered by the BDCs at zero or very low prices; (ii) increased product quality – these services meet consumer preferences in terms of speed and simplicity; and (iii) the evident increase in the degree of innovation. Under this last profile, it is indeed necessary to remember that the BDCs find space in the markets of banking and financial services, also due to the technological limits of traditional intermediaries. Thus, if it is true that the entry of the BDCs could result in a reduction in the business volumes of banks and payment institutions already present in the market, as well as a reduction in their margins, caused by the offer of services at lower fees, it is equally true that antitrust law considers these effects pro-competitive and, therefore, lawful.

Moreover, these assessments would not change even if BDCs were found to be dominant – a fact which is not at all easy to determine – in their core business, that is, even where it is estimated that Google, Amazon and Facebook are companies that enjoy significant market power in the search engine, e-commerce and social network markets. And this because antitrust law does not pursue companies that increase consumer welfare, even when they occupy a dominant position.

Further, the same conclusions about the pro-competitive nature of BDCs' conduct can also be achieved by looking at the reasons why these companies would expand and enrich the range of their services. Respectively – and returning to the three strategies listed above – allowing consumers to enjoy many integrated services addressing a single digital ecosystem according to the 'one-stop-shop' theory is not anti-competitive in itself. Rather, this dynamic could signal that in the future, competition will be consumed between digital platforms and ecosystems and not between individual functions or applications. In other words, the desire to offer users more and more complete, almost totalitarian, experiences could be good evidence of a mere change in the industrial paradigm, before supporting any hypothesis about the existence of an exclusionary conduct detrimental to consumer welfare.

Secondly, the choice to explore every innovative path available in order not to be later outclassed by rival platforms does not (apparently) produce any harm to consumer welfare, in terms of output and market prices, or in terms of variety, quality and degree of innovation in the offer of companies. Therefore, even this strategy as such does not bear any anti-competitive feature.

Finally, even the choice of the BDCs to expand the range of their services in order to increase their data assets cannot be considered as infringing on antitrust law. This choice, in fact, triggers a phenomenon of 'internal growth' of this data that cannot be qualified as anti-competitive, as long as the data are collected due to the preference that consumers give to the services of the BDCs 'to the detriment' of those offered by traditional intermediaries.[7]

Should we, therefore, conclude that there are no (or they cannot be figured out) profiles of competitive complexity connected to the entry of the BDCs in the banking and financial markets?

Actually, it could be observed that the competing companies of the BDCs can never match their informative/competitive advantage: for example, they cannot match their customer base and, therefore, their data assets. And, therefore, it could be noted that these competitors are deprived of the possibility of operating under the same conditions ('same level playing field'). The real crux of the matter, however, would remain the same: antitrust law is not in the best possible position to protect the current and potential competitors of the BDCs, as long as BDCs offer services favoured by consumers. If you want to act on the number, on the plurality of subjects offering banking and financial services, or if you want to equip traditional competitors with equal competitive instruments, it would be better to resort to specific regulations rather than looking for an antitrust intervention.

Furthermore, with reference to the fact that the BDCs would be better than traditional intermediaries because they are preferred by consumers, one could object that such favour is 'biased' because consumers are not being sufficiently informed and /or sufficiently trained to make informed decisions in the environment of Internet. For example, the customization of financial products and services offered in the market could, according to some, weaken and undermine the ability of savers/consumers to compare the different options offered to them (Joint Committee of the European Supervisory Authorities 2016: 22–3). Again, however,

7 A different reasoning should be elaborated in relation to mergers whereby BDCs increase their datasets.

it must be said that antitrust law is not in the best possible position to manage these phenomena. It would be best to invoke the general principles that look at the need to standardize investment proposals. Or, in more general terms, the possibility that consumers make informed and aware choices could be better guaranteed by appealing to the discipline of consumers' protection, to various forms of sensitization of the same, or to the application of rules of transparency and norms to protect privacy.

4. The case for specific antitrust actions

What has just been said about the way in which, in general terms, antitrust law conceptualizes and manages new competitors' market entry does not rule out that, under particular circumstances, antitrust authorities can and must act against whoever is capable of producing an antitrust injury, even if newcomers. Thus, nothing excludes an antitrust intervention against big data companies whose behaviours are, after all, already under the scrutiny of the national and European competition authorities (see European Commission 2017a, 2017b, 2018 and Bundeskartellamt 2017).

On the other hand, so far, the only antitrust cases about new payment systems that have been recorded concern the 'defensive' behaviours of banks. Consider, for example, the Australian case about Apple Pay. In July 2016, four Australian banks asked the Australian Competition and Consumer Commission (ACCC) for the authorization to negotiate jointly against Apple, with the ultimate goal of increasing their bargaining power against the giant US firm. In particular, the four banks wanted to: (i) acquire direct access to the near-field communication (NFC) controller located in Apple's iPhones, in order to offer their own integrated digital wallets to iPhone customers in competition with Apple's digital wallet without any mediation of Apple Pay; and (ii) remove restrictions that Apple imposed on banks preventing them from passing on fees that Apple charges the banks for the use of its digital wallet. The banks argued that being able to engage in the proposed conduct would have increased pricing efficiency, consumer choice and innovation in digital wallets and other mobile applications using near-field communication technology. However, in November 2016, the ACCC rejected the application, meaning each bank needed to reach an individual agreement with Apple to prevent any form of horizontal collusion among banks and too much interference with the innovative path of development of such a young market. For what is more here, the ACCC maintained that, notwithstanding Apple's leading role as to online payments, no joint negotiation was necessary, as banks did not risk being foreclosed from the payment service market just because of Apple's exclusive control on the NFC located in iPhones. Not only did banks already offer competing digital wallets on iPhones without direct access to NFC, but also through their own apps either using Apple Pay payment technology or using NFC tags. Also, banks could reach out to customers by offering digital wallets on the alternative Android platform. Also, the payment system market still included other major payment services, such as credit cards, which banks control.

Furthermore, let us consider another example in relation to the access to account rule as provided for by Directive 2366/2015 on payment services in the internal market (PSD2) (see Scopsi 2019). With the ultimate goal of increasing competition in the retail payment market, this rule allows providers of both payment initiation services (PISPs) and account information services (AISs) to have real-time account data relating to online banks' customers as well real-time access to such accounts by executing payment orders initiated through PISPs' interfaces, on condition that these customers give their explicit consent (Articles 64–8 of PSD2). Thus, the rule enables online banks' customers to choose who will offer them the above services, whether incumbents or newcomers, without worrying about whether the 'chosen' service provider will actually have available the data that it needs to offer the service at stake. In other words, the rule cancels the competitive advantage that banks enjoy for being the platforms on which their customers' data lie, with the ultimate goal of creating a single level playing field for banks and other providers of financial services.[8] Indeed, banks are under obligation to grant such access on a non-discriminatory basis both to PISPs and to AISPs (Article 66 (4)(c) of PSD2).

Now, as said above, antitrust law does not and should not interfere with this regulatory provision. Nevertheless, antitrust authorities should intervene if banks act to undermine the effectiveness of the access to account rule. Indeed, since incumbents retain strong incentives to foreclose new Fintech entrants and the implementation process of the XS2A rule is inherently complex, traditional banking players can easily engage in subtle forms of anti-competitive practices, which risk frustrating the potential of the XS2A rule. For example, in 2016 the Bundeskartellamt – Germany's Competition Authority – found anti-competitive certain terms and conditions that the German Banking Industry Committee imposed on online banking customers (see Bundeskartellamt 2016a, 2016b). Namely, these customers were not allowed to use their PIN and TAN in non-bank payment systems,

8 See the Competition and Markets Authority website: *Retail Banking Market Investigation*, https://www.gov.uk/cma-cases/review-of-banking-for-small-and-medium-sized-businesses-smes-in-the-uk.

although such a ban was not meant to shelter banks' security systems. The German competition authority therefore concluded that the ban served to increase customers' switching costs, with the ultimate goal of preventing non-bank providers of payment services from entering the market, despite the regulatory provision. Equally, in October 2017 the European Commission carried out some inspections in the offices of European banking associations in Poland and the Netherlands, looking to find evidence of alleged anti-competitive practices aimed at blocking non-bank-owned providers of financial services from gaining access to the account data of customers who authorized it (Europan Commission 2017c).

5. Business opportunities for banks

To be sure, the above antitrust actions do not stand for the idea that banks are doomed to succumb to big data or Fintech companies.

On the contrary, in Australia, three of the four banks mentioned above have announced a new joint venture named Beem which is charged with developing a mobile wallet for iOS and Android users, with the ultimate goal of creating an 'industry-wide payment solution' open to the customers of any bank, including organizations outside of the trio. In other words, these banks have decided to develop their own competitive-friendly solution to stay in the market and get around Apple at the same time (EBA 2018: 24–34).

Likewise, thanks to the access to account rule, banks have the opportunity to take full advantage of their gatekeeper role by positioning themselves as platforms. Similar to what Apple did by opening its operating systems, financial companies that want to gain (and maintain) a leading position in such a new ecosystem would need to provide APIs to outside developers, who can then build new products on the banks' platforms (Brainard 2017: 6). In this way, banks could group, on one side, customers and, on the other side, third-party service providers such as, primarily, AISs and PISs, to exploit then the indirect network effects existing between the number of banks' customers and the number of Fintech services compatible with banks' accounts (Zachariadis and Ozcan 2017). In other words, Open Banking is laying the foundation of a new business model, a two-sided business model, based on banking platforms acting as intermediaries for both account holders and Fintech companies and generating potential value for both sides (Colangelo and Borgogno 2018).

More in general, today banks often complain that their datasets are less differentiated and varied than the datasets of big data companies. However, thanks to Article 20 of the GDPR, this feature is not doomed to last. Indeed, pursuant to Article 20 of the GDPR, each person has the right to have returned to them personal data they have provided to a company or organization on the basis of consent or contract and has the right to have that data transmitted without hindrance from one controller to another (even directly where technically feasible). Thus, owing to the data portability right, Internet users are allowed to choose how to manage their data: they can transfer data between online providers; they are able to give their profiles, such as their past search history, to whoever will use them to offer value-added personalized services; and in addition, they are capable of exerting influence over the trading and commercialization of their data. Now, in such a scenario, nothing prevents banks from developing some commercial solutions whereby their customers transfer their data to banks in exchange for additional services or lower prices. In other words, in the current data economy, banks are not doomed to keep on working on their own data: they can increase the variety as well as the quality of their datasets to the develop new products and services.

Concluding remarks

The entrance as such of new players in the markets for banking and financial services cannot fall within the scope of a specific antitrust rule, especially because antitrust law does not equal a piece of regulation, aimed at governing a given industry, but rather envisages targeted interventions justified by specific circumstances.

To be sure, this state of affairs does not exclude that an antitrust authority can act against a BDC undertaking a practice harming the good operation of the market, for example, limiting output or increasing market price in the short-run, and/or decreasing quality, variety or the pace of innovation in the long-run. However, first, this should be assessed on a case-by-case basis. Second, the antitrust cases recorded so far have rather regarded banks' behaviours as aimed at increasing newcomers' costs of entry.

Nevertheless, the very same data economy provides even traditional incumbents with new business opportunities and strategies. Consider, as a way of example, the case of banks acting as new intermediary platforms between traditional customers and tech firms, or the case of banks willing to increase their data booty, by fully exploiting individuals' rights to data portability.

References

Bansal, Sukriti et al. (2015), "How the Payments Industry is Being Disrupted", in *McKinsey Articles*, November, http://bit.ly/2hTH84G.

Brainard, Lael (2017), *Where Do Banks Fit in the Fintech Stack?*, Speech at Northwestern Kellogg Public–Private Interface Conference on 'New Developments in Consumer Finance: Research and Practice', 28 April, https://www.federalreserve.gov/newsevents/speech/brainard20170428a.htm.

Bundeskartellamt (2016a), Decision in case B4-71-10, 29 June, https://www.bundeskartellamt.de/SharedDocs/Entscheidung/DE/Entscheidungen/Kartellverbot/2016/B4-71-10.html.

Bundeskartellamt (2016b), *Restriction of Online Payment Services by German Banking Industry in Violation of Competition Law*, 5 July, https://www.bundeskartellamt.de/SharedDocs/Meldung/EN/Pressemitteilungen/2016/05_07_2016_Sofortüberweisung.html.

Bundeskartellamt (2017), *Preliminary Assessment in Facebook Proceeding: Facebook's Collection and Use of Data from Third-Party Sources is Abusive*, 19 December, https://www.bundeskartellamt.de/SharedDocs/Meldung/EN/Pressemitteilungen/2017/19_12_2017_Facebook.html.

Colangelo, Giuseppe and Oscar Borgogno (2018), 'Data, Innovation and Transatlantic Competition in Finance: The Case of the Access to Account Rule', in *European Union Law Working Papers*, No. 35, https://law.stanford.edu/?p=261995.

Directive (EU) 2015/2366 of 25 November 2015 on Payment Services in the Internal Market, amending Directives 2002/65/EC, 2009/110/EC and 2013/36/EU and Regulation (EU) No. 1093/2010, and repealing Directive 2007/64/EC (PSD2), http://data.europa.eu/eli/dir/2015/2366/oj.

European Banking Authority (2017), *Discussion Paper on the EBA's Approach to Financial Technology (FinTech)* (EBA/DP/2017/02), 4 August, https://eba.europa.eu/-/eba-publishes-a-discussion-paper-on-its-approach-to-fintech.

European Banking Authority (2018), *EBA Report on the Impact of Fintech on Incumbent Credit Institutions' Business Models*, 3 July, https://eba.europa.eu/-/eba-assesses-risks-and-opportunities-from-fintech-and-its-impact-on-incum bents-business-models.

European Commission (2017a), Decision in case AT.39740: Google Search (Shopping), 27 June, http://ec.europa.eu/competition/elojade/isef/case_details.cfm?proc_code=1_39740.

European Commission (2017b), Decision on State aid SA.38944: Aid to Amazon-Luxembourg, 4 October, http://ec.europa.eu/competition/elojade/isef/case_details.cfm?proc_code=3_SA_38944.

European Commission (2017c), *Fact Sheet: Antitrust: Commission Confirms Unannounced Inspections Concerning Access To Bank Account Information by Competing Services*, 6 October, http://europa.eu/rapid/press-release_MEMO-17-3761_en.htm.

European Commission (2018), Decision in case AT.40099: Google Android, 18 July, http://ec.europa.eu/competition/elojade/isef/case_details.cfm?proc_code=1_40099.

Joint Committee of the European Supervisory Authorities (2016), *Joint Committee Discussion Paper on the Use of Big Data by Financial Institutions*, JC 2016/86, https://www.esma.europa.eu/node/82487.

Kottasova, Ivana (2017), "You Can Now Transfer Money Internationally Through Facebook", in *CNN Money*, 21 February, http://cnnmon.ie/2kHaPdn.

Maggiolino, Mariateresa (2018), *I big data e il diritto antitrust*, Milano, Egea.

Petit, Nicholas (2016), *Technology Giants, the 'Moligopoly' Hypothesis and Holistic Competition: A Primer*, Paper presented at the Bruegel seminar 'Digital Platforms: A Policy and Research Agenda', Brussels, 20 October, http://bruegel.org/wp-content/uploads/2016/10/Tech-Giants-The-Moligopoly-Hypothezis-and-Holitic-Competition-A-Primer-PETIT-20-10-16-1-1.pdf.

Scopsi, Martina (2019), 'The Expansion of Big Data Companies in the Financial Services Industry, and EU Regulation', in *IAI Papers*, No. 19|06 (March), https://www.iai.it/en/node/10163.

Zachariadis, Markos and Pinar Ozcan (2017), "The API Economy and Digital Transformation in Financial Services: The Case of Open Banking", in *SWIFT Institute Working Papers*, No. 2016-001 (June), https://swiftinstitute.org/?p=1964.

Fabrizio Virtuani[1]

Focus 5: Information Technology Innovations, Tech Giants and the Fintech Industry

1. Recent information technology innovations

New technologies and the availability of enormous amounts of data are reshaping not only business models, but also the way we make business and elaborate strategies, increasing more and more the pace of change. They have changed the way we think, reducing the importance of gut instinct or 'business sense' and encouraging a more rational, empirical and quicker decision-making process, through the power of data-driven analysis. They are constantly pushing to redefine the competitive lines, challenging the incumbent business models and helping the emersion of new competitors. They are revealing and helping to create new markets, previously unknown or irrelevant, thanks also to ever-faster innovation: with mobile and Internet-enabled new technologies, companies are able to experiment and introduce new products and services at a pace and scale we have never seen before.

As a result, in the last fifteen years, 52 per cent of S&P 500 companies have disappeared, being acquired, merged or declared bankrupt (Perry 2017); and, like in the recent past, in the near future we will see disruption in many businesses, arriving with a very typical pattern experienced in the recent corporate crisis.[2] Initially, gradual signals of the coming disaster arise in twelve to eighteen months, with the stock value decreasing, but then, suddenly, the catastrophic effects arrive in four to five months, with the stock value collapsing very quickly and not recovering. The weak signals therefore should never be underestimated: new emerging technologies need to be carefully monitored, understood and evaluated, to capture all the possible implications for the different industries and existing business models, especially where there are large profit pools and huge markets that can be attacked.

Some of the recent information technology (IT) innovations that are having a strong impact on the financial industry and that we will briefly illustrate here

---

1 Fabrizio Virtuani is Adjunct Professor in Digital Transformations at LUISS Business School.

2 For example, Blackberry vs Apple iPhone, Blockbuster vs Netflix, Hertz vs Uber.

are the following: big data/just data, analytics and MarTech; artificial intelligence (AI), machine learning and deep learning; distributed ledger technologies and blockchains; cloud computing and containerization (for example, Docker).

Big data/just data, analytics and MarTech

Big data is a term initially applied to very large data sets, too complex to be treated with traditional database software applications, and include technologies for capturing data, data storage, data analysis, search, sharing, transfer, visualization, querying, updating, information privacy and security. The term 'big data' was originally associated with three key concepts: high data volume; large variety (and low structuring); and velocity (of acquisition or change). Traditional relational database management systems, statistics and other software packages used to collect, analyse and store data often had difficulty handling big data, sometimes requiring massive parallel software and huge servers.

New software tools, architectures and systems have been developed to treat big data, such as flat file systems, dedicated machines and in-memory databases. Nowadays as the amount of produced and collected data continues to increase, for example in fields like genomics, biology, medicine, physics and meteorology, we seldom use the term referring to the size of the data sets, rather, the current usage tends to refer to predictive analytics, user behaviour analytics or other advanced data analytics methods that extract value from data. Therefore, we use the term 'just data' and we talk more of 'analytics' – software tools for the discovery, interpretation and communication of meaningful patterns in data and application of those patterns to effective decision-making – and 'MarTech' – software applications and technology platforms for collecting and managing data for marketing purposes, like user profiling, advertising targeting, business insights and audience analytics.

Artificial intelligence, machine learning and deep learning

AI refers to intelligence demonstrated by machines, when a machine imitates cognitive functions usually associated with human minds, such as 'learning' and 'problem solving'. Traditional AI research problems include reasoning, knowledge representation, planning, learning, natural language processing, perception and the ability to move and manipulate objects. The main AI approaches are statistical methods, computational intelligence and symbolic AI. The tools used are search and optimization, logic, probabilistic methods for uncertain reasoning, classifiers and statistical learning methods, and artificial neural networks.

In recent years we have seen many advances in the artificial neural networks, thanks to the exponential increase in the computational power of central processing units (CPUs) and graphics processing units (GPUs). In particular, the most recent and promising developments have been in:

1) Machine learning, with algorithms and mathematical models that computer systems use to progressively improve their performance on a specific task, starting from sample or training data, and making predictions or decisions without being explicitly programmed to perform the task. The main applications are email filtering, network intruder detection, computer vision, computational statistics, mathematical optimization and data mining.
2) Deep learning, also known as deep structured learning or hierarchical learning, which is a particular subset of machine learning methods, that are based on representations and inferences on learning huge data sets, and not on task-specific algorithms. The main applications are in automatic speech recognition, image recognition, visual art processing (like style-period identification and imitation, artificial images generation, and so on), natural language processing (sentiment analysis, information retrieval, spoken language understanding, machine translation, writing-style recognition, text classification, etc.), new drug discovery and toxicology, customer relationship management applications, recommendation systems, medical and bio-informatics, healthcare, mobile advertising, image restoration, financial fraud detection, cybersecurity and military applications.

Distributed ledger technologies and blockchains

A distributed ledger (or shared ledger) is a geographically spread platform across multiple sites that provides the ability to store and reach consensus on replicated, shared and synchronized digital data, with no central administrator or centralized data storage. The distributed ledger technology (DLT) requires therefore a peer-to-peer network and a consensus algorithm to ensure replication across nodes. The most well-known DLT is the blockchain system, which allows untrusted parties (nodes of the blockchain) to reach agreement (consensus) on a common digital history. Having a common digital history is important because digital assets and transactions are in theory easily faked and/or duplicated; blockchain technology solves this problem without using a trusted intermediary. The main applications are the mining, exchange, storage and validation of digital certificates, cryptocurrencies, smart contracts, banking settlements and online voting.

Cloud computing and containerization (for example, Docker)

Cloud computing is an IT infrastructure that allows the rapid and easy provisioning of delocalized, shared and configurable computer system resources and higher-level services, either from the Internet (public cloud, available concurrently to many different customers) or from a proprietary or dedicated datacentre (private cloud, dedicated to a single customer). Cloud computing has been made possible thanks to the availability of high-capacity networks, low-cost computers and data storage clusters, and most importantly the widespread adoption of hardware virtualization, permitting the sharing of physical server resources to achieve economies of scale. Cloud computing allows companies to avoid or minimize up-front IT infrastructure costs, to develop and deliver applications faster, to ease application management, to reduce or cancel hardware and basic software maintenance and to enable the rapid IT resources adjustment to meet fluctuating and unpredictable demand.

Containerization (also best known as a specific software application denominated 'Docker') is a software programme that performs operating-system-level virtualization, inside a single operating system kernel, usually in the cloud. It runs software packages called 'containers', isolated from each other, that bundle their own application, tools, libraries, configuration files, databases, and so on. As all containers are run by a single operating system kernel, they are much more lightweight than virtual machines; they are created from 'images' that specify their exact contents, and the images are often created by modifying or combining standard images downloaded from public repositories. Therefore, a single virtual machine can run several containers simultaneously (for example, a typical-use case involves running from five containers per host to ten or more). Containers simplify the creation of highly distributed and concurrent systems by allowing multiple applications, tasks and processes to run autonomously on a single physical machine or across multiple virtual machines. Moreover, the deployment of new nodes is much quicker and can be performed as the need arises, allowing a higher flexibility of deployment and speed of scaling.

2. Tech giants' new technologies adoption and applications

Tech giants (Alphabet-Google, Amazon, Apple, Facebook and Microsoft) are the world five biggest companies for market capitalization.[3] Only in 2008 the

3 See Financial Times website: *Markets Data: Equities*, https://markets.ft.com/data/equities.

ranking was very different:[4] Exxon, PetroChina, Wal-Mart, China Mobile, Procter&Gamble (followed by ICBC, Microsoft, AT&T, Johnson & Johnson, General Electric). Tech giants are investing heavily to build competencies in the new emerging technologies, both to offer additional products and services to their customers and to protect themselves from possible threats coming from their competitors' potential technology-induced disruptions.

Alphabet-Google

Thanks to its strong search engine technologies, spanning from hardware to operating systems, programming languages and massively transactional software applications, Alphabet is a leader in many new technologies: big data, analytics, MarTech applications (86 per cent of Alphabet's revenues in 2017 came from performance advertising, through user clicks using Adsense and AdWords, and brand advertising) and cloud computing, the latter with mixed results, excellent in personal-information-management applications, with lower success in B2B IT services (behind Amazon AWS and Microsoft Azure).

Alphabet's main new technologies investment focus is on artificial intelligence, machine learning and deep learning (through its subsidiary Deep Mind and also with the Google Brain team inside Google), with a vision that says 'we are evolving from a mobile-first to an AI-first world'; it is also focused heavily on speech recognition and natural language processing for its Google Assistant, Google Translate and many other products (smart speakers, digital car, smart home and wearables) and services. New products will be aimed at task assistance, like Duplex, a future capability for the assistant that can carry out phone calls on a user's behalf, or radar-based gesture sensing and data transmission to control devices.

Other Alphabet key investments are in healthcare, biotechnology and life sciences (through Calico and Verily), cybersecurity (through Chronicle and Jigsaw), geothermal heating (through Dandelion Energy), 'moonshot' technologies (defined as technologies at the intersection of a big problem, a radical solution, and a breakthrough technology – through X Development, previously Google X), and in many other initiatives through GV (previously Google Venture) and CapitalG (later-stage and growth equity investments).

Besides search engines and mobile (through Android), the other key market priority for Alphabet is cloud computing and storage (regaining competitiveness through serverless computing, also known as function-as-a-service or FaaS, that

4 Ibid.

allows businesses to pay for resources per function rather than paying for pre-defined computing capacity and storage).

Other significant markets being addressed are Internet of Things and edge computing, content delivery networks on optical fibres, mobile payments, medical devices, digital health, healthcare IT, digital advertising, gaming, autonomous vehicles, shared mobility, logistics and supply chain, smart home devices, quantum computing and digital assistants.

Amazon

Rising from being a Seattle-based Internet bookstore, Amazon has grown in five major industries: retail; logistics; consumer technology; cloud computing; and most recently, media and entertainment. In particular, besides the retail core business, Amazon has invested heavily in cloud technologies and has created a very successful enterprise cloud business, Amazon Web Services.

Amazon has also the largest share of product search and is gaining traction in advertising: Amazon dominates product search, outpacing Google, and while Google and Facebook still dominate the online advertising market, Amazon has the third largest share of digital advertising revenue.

Amazon's next focus is on AI and machine learning, to maintain its relevance and edge over its competition; it is investing especially in AI-as-a-service, creating basic AI tools for its cloud computing and developer community, and pushing more and more to become a platform company.

Another important investment sector is healthcare, in particular cancer detection and genomics, with massive data and processing needs.

Voice, virtual assistants and natural language processing will continue to be a focus for Amazon, creating a valuable ecosystem around its Alexa voice computing platform: software development kits (SDKs) that allow third-party developers to build skills for the AI assistant and other manufacturers of hardware to integrate the Alexa assistant into their products; new interfaces, like gesture controls; GPS tracking; smart home security cameras; and smart doorbells.

Also, Amazon aims to grow its market share in physical retail and consumer goods in general, with Amazon Go, its cashier-less convenience store.

Finally, Amazon is exploiting its strong technologies and market dominance to expand into the financial services industry.

Apple

Starting from a very strong position in consumer hardware (smartphones, tablets, personal computers, and so on) and with very strong ecosystems in contents like music, videos, books and in payments, Apple is exploring its next big thing in spaces like healthcare IT, augmented reality, intelligent and battery-efficient wearables, autonomous driving software and technologies like light and ranging detection sensor and smaller and lighter batteries, home entertainment and smart homes. In the AI, machine learning and natural language processing domain, after an initial lead with the 2011 launch of the Siri virtual assistant, Apple has ceded ground to Google, Amazon and Microsoft, but it has very strong internal capacity to design AI-optimized chips, therefore something very secretive could be in the works.

Facebook

Facebook seems more focused on consolidating and rationalizing the acquisitions made, like WhatsApp and especially Instagram, than on innovations and technology; also, the Oculus VR virtual reality acquisition is getting less attention than in the past, while its strongest focus is on monetizing the social networks, through advertising, measurements and pricing strategy. Due to the recent problems, much attention is being devoted to privacy and compliance policies, using encryption and potentially blockchain technology to better protect privacy.

The interest in blockchain technology is demonstrated by some significant events: in May 2018 Facebook announced its largest reorganization ever, creating a blockchain group run by former Messenger head (and ex-PayPal president) David Marcus and moving Instagram VP of Product Kevin Weil to the project; in June 2018 it reversed the previous ban on cryptocurrency ads; in August 2018 David Marcus stepped down from the Coinbase board, citing a conflict of interest. Having also patented a virtual credit transfer system with real and digital exchange rates, and having 2 billion users and Facebook Connect single-sign-on that constitute the largest identity provider worldwide, Facebook seems to be exploring the building of coin incentives for e-commerce, micropayments for services and content creators, banking apps, cryptocurrency exchanges, identity tech for apps, and even a branchless bank.

Microsoft

Microsoft has been a pioneer in the cloud industry, developing a complete offer of cloud platforms, solutions and services, but as the cloud industry is becoming more commoditized, Microsoft is developing its own AI products and solutions, enriching its cloud platform, to differentiate from the competitors and attract corporate customers. Also, the customer segment focus has shifted a lot from the past, moving from consumers and small businesses to primarily enterprises, becoming the largest enterprise technology company. After the acquisition of the LinkedIn professional social network and GitHub software source code repository, Microsoft main technology innovation focus seem to be on low-latency and edge cloud services, robotic process and workflow automation, AI application programme interfaces and smart devices with flexible displays.

3. Financial industry transformation due to the new technologies

Besides the tech giants, financial industry top players are also beginning to invest significantly to define, adopt and exploit the new technologies, also hiring top executives from the Big Tech players or from the most advanced universities and building strong in-house tech teams and competencies (for example, Goldman Sachs and JP Morgan in 2018 hired artificial intelligence top managers and experts from Amazon, Google and Carnegie Mellon) (Morrell 2018).

More generally, the financial industry is undergoing a profound transformation, with Fintechs (startups, technology companies or even initiatives inside traditional banks) exploiting technological innovations and the digitalization of financial services to develop innovative products, services and technology-enabled business models in the different segments of the financial industry:

1) Lending: crowdfunding technologies, marketplace lending and alternative underwriting platforms.
2) Regulation: regtechs, with software and software-as-a-service applications for audit, risk management and regulatory compliance.
3) Personal finance: software tools to automatically manage bills, receipts, payments and track personal and/or credit accounts.
4) Payments/billing: payments processing, card developing and issuing (including dematerialized cards), subscription services management and billing software tools.
5) Insurance: digital selling insurance, claim management, software tools and data analytics for insurers and reinsurers.
6) Capital markets: sales and trading analysis, software and infrastructure tools for financial institutions.
7) Wealth management: investment and wealth management platforms and analytics tools.
8) Money transfer/remittances: international money transfers and tracking platforms and applications.
9) Mortgage/real estate: mortgage lending, digitization and financing platforms.

In the first half of 2018, Fintech financing deals from venture capital funds (including those owned by tech giants) reached a record high of $26 billion in 732 deals, compared to $15–18 billion in each of the years 2015–17. The Fintech 'unicorns' worldwide (companies with a market capitalization of more than $1 billion) are 29 and are cumulatively valued at more than $84 billion; there are none in Italy, only four in Europe, of which three are in the UK and one in Sweden, eighteen in the USA, one in Brazil, four in China and two in India.

The situation in Italy is in a very primordial state, with many small initiatives, the majority of which are in a design or prototype stage, that still have to prove their value-generation capability and need to be supported and reinforced.

A December 2017 Banca d'Italia report, 'Fintech in Italy: A survey on the adoption of technological innovations applied to financial services', analysed 283 'Fintech initiatives' in progress, with a cumulated cost of 135 million euro, a very small amount considering the huge ICT investments of the Italian banks (Banca d'Italia 2017). It looks even smaller if we take into account that 92 per cent of this amount is spent by the twelve biggest banks, designated as 'significant institutions' (Carige, MontePaschi, BPM, BPER, Banca Popolare di Sondrio, Barclays Bank, Credito Emiliano, ICCREA, Intesa Sanpaolo, Mediobanca, Unicredit and UBI) and therefore it is less than 3 per cent of their cumulated annual IT expenses.

What is even worse is that nearly 70 per cent of the amount categorized as Fintech investments is in reality spent in the development of ICT systems that are quite traditional, and should be considered as 'IT renewal'. Forty-nine per cent are 'customer services automation' (which includes now widespread and standard technologies, such as offers comparison portals, customer accounts information services and, maybe the only more innovative solutions, automated CRM services with AI solutions like chatbox and automated financial consultancy with robo-advisors). Twenty-seven per cent are generic 'support technologies' (which are innovative but their implementations look more like experiments, not clearly connected to well-defined applications: big data; artificial intelligence; cloud computing; open application programming interfaces; and Internet of Things), 7 per cent are 'technologies for contracts and remote operations' (that are now standard applications such as electronic identity management and/or remote recognition of the customer, like SPID, used for the subscription of financial services), 4 per cent are payment systems, 0.4 per cent on distributed ledger systems (blockchain), and 13 per cent for generic 'others'.

Looking at the Fintech startups, in Italy there are about 235 new ventures that offer financial products and services, including 'pure tech' initiatives, more transversal but with potential financial applications (PwC and NetConsulting cube 2018). Of the overall startups, 8 per cent are InsureTech, 30 per cent are crowdfunding, 20 per cent wealth and asset management, 20 per cent payment, 10 per cent lending, 7 per cent financial security and the rest are trading and capital market solutions. Yet all those initiatives together collected only 30 million euro investments in 2017. In Italy, therefore, much remains to be done.

4. Tech giants' potential advantages in the Fintech industry due to their technology and market dominance

The complete mastery of the new technologies by the tech giants (Apple, Google, Microsoft, Amazon, Facebook, as well as Alibaba) and their enormous and loyal customer base make them potentially also strong Fintechs and therefore formidable possible competitors in the financial sector. Amazon and Alibaba are presently the most active, and we will analyse further their initiatives, while Alphabet-Google and Apple are focusing more on mobile payments (Android Pay, Google Wallet, Apple Pay), and Facebook on blockchain applications and peer-to-peer payments in Messenger (in the USA, the UK and France only).

Amazon has adapted financial products and services, tailoring them for its merchants and final customers. The present Amazon main initiatives are:

1) Payments: Amazon Flexible Payments Service (web service API to allow the transfer of money between computers or humans); Amazon WebPay (former TextPayMe); Amazon Pay, evolved into a digital wallet for customers and a payments network for merchants, with more than 33 million customers in 170 countries; and Amazon Go, introducing new payment technological innovations, like facial recognition.
2) Cash: Amazon Cash as a cash depository, with no fees to shop on Amazon; Amazon Allowance, where with parental consent, children can set up their own Amazon accounts and make purchases using their allowance, and parents can allocate recurring funds to their child's account and get the added control of overseeing what their children purchase; and partnership with CoinStar ATMs.
3) Lending: Amazon Lending is creating a strong relationship with platform merchants, reaching the amount of $3 billion of small and medium businesses loans to 20,000 firms in the USA, UK and Japan; Amazon Lending is trying to partner with banks so they can use their expertise to take and manage the bulk of the credit risk; Amazon Card for online and everyday usage; and Amazon Reload as a reloadable digital debit card for Prime members.
4) Insurance: Amazon Protect as a product insurance white label in Europe.

But Amazon's strategy in financial services still seems to be strictly connected to its core strategy: increase the number of merchants on Amazon, and enable each merchant to sell more; increase the number of customers on Amazon, and enable each customer to spend more; reduce buy/sell friction, building and launching tools aimed at making its marketplace easier to transact in for existing customers and merchants.

Alibaba, with Alipay, has created in China a modern gateway to an ecosystem of financial services; Ant Financial's valuation is now the number 10 market cap of leading global banks:

1) Payments: Alipay is now a mobile wallet with more than 520 million users and 110 million partners across 15 countries.
2) Wealth management: Yu'e Bao is the largest money market fund in the world, which invests spare change from Alipay wallets, managing $233 billion at the end of 2017; Ant Fortune is a marketplace for other Ant Financial and third-party financial products, with 330 million users at the end of 2017.
3) Insurance: Ant Insurance Service has nearly 400 million users and is seeing premium growth of 43 per cent YoY; Ant Financial's marketplace has eighty-plus insurance companies selling thousands of products.
4) Credit score: Zhima Credit creates a credit score based, among other factors, on social networks and payments history, with about 260 million users at the end of Q1 2017.
5) Consumer lending: Ant Credit Pay is Ant's consumer credit offering, with 100 million active users and $95 billion lent to consumers through Q1 2017; Ant Cash Now allows Alipay users to borrow funds quickly, based on user risk profiles.

The technological and market power of the tech giants seen from the financial industry is certainly scary but, overall, the tech giants' financial services don't look like being head-on attacks on the traditional financial players. The tech giants have enormous cash resources and technological competences that could allow them to enter any sector they decide to compete in, but again, their financial services seem to be carefully selected, designed and implemented add-ons to their core business, to complement it and to strengthen it, increasing their customers lock-in and defending therefore their customer base from possible attacks coming from the other competing tech giants.

Concluding remarks

In conclusion, perhaps technological giants do not constitute (yet?) a real threat to finance big players, not because they do not have the means to enter the financial industrial sector, but because they seem not to be interested in completely replacing existing players: they instead add financial services (like Amazon and Alibaba), such as digital payments and NFC, cash wallets, lending and insurance to complement their core business, to strengthen it and protect it from possible attacks by the other top technological players.

Fintech startups seem to be a more dangerous threat to financial incumbents, also because they are entering the age of scale as investment flows into these companies. Fintech investment has seen a big shift toward mega-rounds into perceived winners, as demonstrated by the top venture-capital-backed Fintech financings rounds in 2018: Creditkarma (free credit scores) $500 million; Robinhood (free trades) $363 million; CGTZ (debt investment portal) $359 million; Revolut (free money transfer) $250 million; Atom Bank (mobile-only lender) $207 million; and many other over $100 million financing rounds, like Oscar Health (health insurance company), N26 (mobile-only bank), NUBank (free credit cards), Black Fish (Internet consumer finance platform), Circle Internet Financial Corporation (crypto-finance company), Tandem Money Corporation (digital retail bank) and eToro (investment social network).

The Fintech startups are offering new and well-designed products and services with new revenue models, offering more for less, ultimately free to the end user. The push towards free will open up existing and previously inaccessible financial products to a much wider pool of customers. These emerging companies generally don't attack incumbent players head-on on all the existing services, but rather focus on very specific verticals.

Financial big players, on the other hand, must equip themselves quickly from the technological point of view because they cannot afford to wait for the moves of technological giants or Fintech startups: without internal skills they would not have sufficient response capacity to compete at a speed, which they are not used to. Furthermore, they must quickly decide on the technological strategy to be adopted in the various segments, among 'build', 'buy' or 'partner':

1) Build, for those digital systems and core services where there are already good internal skills, infrastructure and strong medium-term leadership capabilities; unfortunately, however, the 'not invented here' syndrome can be very dangerous, because, according to the most recent statistics, the internal development

time of new technologies can be higher than twelve to twenty-four months in 60 per cent of cases, and 80 per cent of the initiatives fail.

2) Buy, where the internal competences are not many, and the acquisition targets can be easily integrated with the existing infrastructure and company culture (very often the targets are chosen and used more to acquire new skills than for the products they bring with themselves).

   Partner, where the deal is convenient for both players, allows the strengthening or protecion of the competitive positioning and serves to complete the catalogue of products and services in areas not strictly core for the future.

3) In any case, in the financial sector, digital technologies cannot be relegated to the second hierarchical line of reporting, or to captive companies or outsourcing consortia: digital is core business, and future survival and success depend on it.

References

Banca d'Italia (2017), *Fintech in Italia. Indagine conoscitiva sull'adozione delle innovazioni tecnologiche applicate ai servizi finanziari*, December, http://www.bancaditalia.it/media/notizia/fact-finding-exercise-on-fintech-adoption.

Morrell, Alex (2018), 'Goldman Sachs Made a Big Hire from Amazon to Lead Its Artificial-Intelligence Efforts', in *Business Insider*, 3 April.

Perry, Mark J. (2017), 'Fortune 500 Firms 1955 v. 2017: Only 60 Remain, Thanks to the Creative Destruction that Fuels Economic Prosperity', in *AEI Carpe Diem*, 20 October, http://www.aei.org/publication/fortune-500-firms-1955-v-2017-only-12-remain-thanks-to-the-creative-destruction-that-fuels-economic-prosperity.

PwC and NetConsulting cube (2018), *Le aziende del FinTech in Italia*, https://www.pwc.com/it/it/industries/fintech/docs/2017-fintech-report.pdf.

Nicolò Romani and Giancarlo Sfolcini[1]

Focus 6: Data Sovereignty: The European Way to Foster Competition in the Digital Economy

'When a new technology arises, the Americans do business with it, the Chinese copy it and the Europeans regulate it' (Alexandre 2017). Made by Emma Marcegaglia[2] in Davos in 2016, this statement would appear to juxtapose a reactive, bureaucratic image of the 'old continent' against American exuberance and surmised Chinese opportunism. But assuming a different point of view, it highlights the attention paid in Europe to the search for a balance between economic growth and safeguarding citizens' rights, which cannot occur in the absence of a solid and effective regulatory framework. This is also the basis for a developmental model which has made the European Union a market of over 500 million citizens enjoying a unique combination of high per capita incomes and a low inequality index.

Figure 20: World by GDP and Gini Index.

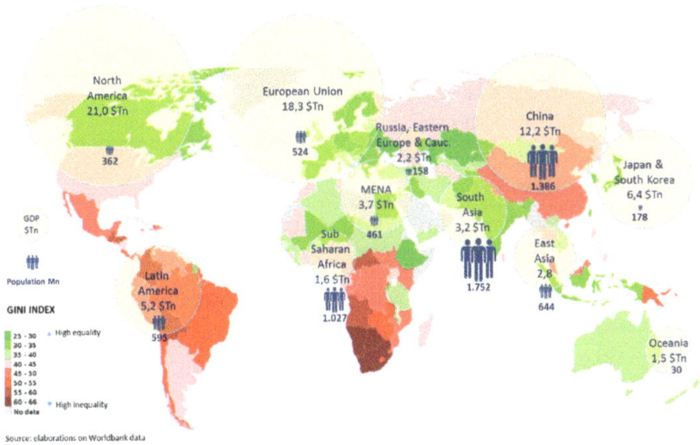

Source: Authors' elaboration from World Bank data.

1 Nicolò Romani is Head of Innovation at SIA and member of the Italian AssoFintech Executive Board. Giancarlo Sfolcini is an Innovation Specialist at SIA.

2 Italian entrepreneur and former president of Confindustria, the main association representing manufacturing and service companies in Italy (she was the youngest person and the first woman in that role). Chairman of ENI since 2014.

Considered from this perspective, the General Data Protection Regulation (GDPR) is nothing other than the practical implementation of Article 8 of the European Union's Charter of Fundamental Rights,[3] despite certain attempts to label it as a 'protectionist' response to the great technological firms (primarily American – the so-called Big Tech firms).

1. Data-driven business models

The use of personal data has a distinct relevance for Big Tech firms, commonly associated with the online world domain, whose business models differ profoundly one from the other.

Table 2: Big tech firms by core business.

	Current core business	**Dependence of core business on personal data processing**
Google (US)	Online advertising / cloud services	High
Amazon (US)	E-commerce and cloud services	Medium
Facebook (US)	Online advertising	High
Apple (US)	Innovative devices (mainly consumer oriented), digital media, cloud services	Low
Microsoft (US)	Individual productivity software and cloud services (*)	Low
Alibaba (China)	E-commerce and financial services	Medium
Tencent (China)	E-commerce, portals, messaging and payments (WeChat)	Medium

Note: * With the acquisition of Skype and LinkedIn, Microsoft has gained a relevant role also in the social media arena.

It should be highlighted that Apple, Microsoft and Amazon have, in the final analysis, a relatively 'traditional' business model: the first two had been selling devices and software well before the days of the Internet[4] (even if they are both striving to

3 1. Everyone has the right to the protection of personal data concerning them. 2. This data must be processed fairly for specified purposes and on the basis of the consent of the person concerned or some other legitimate basis laid down by law. Everyone has right of access to data collected concerning them and the right to have it rectified.

4 Remember they were founded respectively in 1975 and 1976.

get a relevant position in cloud-based services), while catalogue-based distance sales date back to 1872, more than a century before Amazon (and Alibaba). The Internet 'simply' gave them a 'power multiplier' (although with plenty of zeros).

Figure 21: Two-sided market logical model.

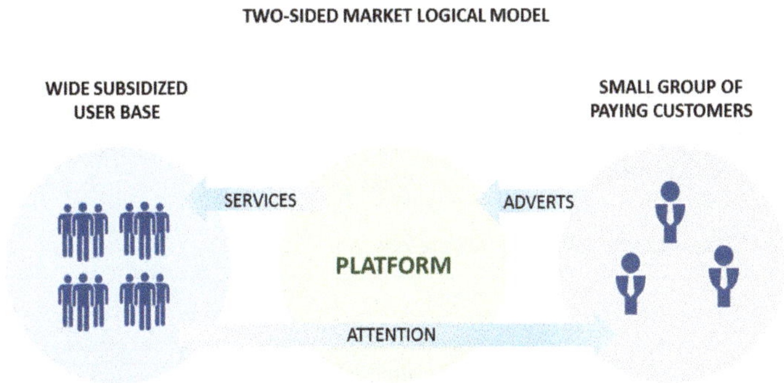

The cases of Google and Facebook, just to consider two of the best-known brands, are to some extent different, as they applied to the digital world the concept of a 'two-sided market': the business model of platforms which generate value (and profits) by facilitating interaction between two different interest groups without a direct relationship between them being established. These two firms have, in practice, made use of the commercial TV model in which one of the two sides is made up of a user base that is as wide as possible, to whom services are provided free of charge (or strongly subsidized), in order to capture their attention which is 'sold' to advertisers on the other side of the system.

As compared to TV, Facebook and Google also had two considerable advantages:

1) With no need to build a distributed technological infrastructure (making use of the connectivity supplied by Internet providers – that earned them an initial label of 'over-the-top' operators), they have thus been able to concentrate their investments on services.
2) Providing interactive services to a global market, they have the possibility to collect data at individual level.

They have thus been able to build an extraordinary analysis capacity[5] enabling them to personalise advertising messages to practically every individual user. This ability has enabled them to offer personalized services (based on geo-localization, for example) even to small- to medium-scale firms, intercepting a 'long tail' whose ability to find space on traditional media is very limited. Companies like Facebook, moreover, took advantage of the active (and generally free) participation of users who have shared highly profitable information and data without themselves earning any direct advantage other than visibility.[6]

The relationship between operating income and revenues represents the effectiveness of this model well.

Figure 22: Companies by operating income/revenue.

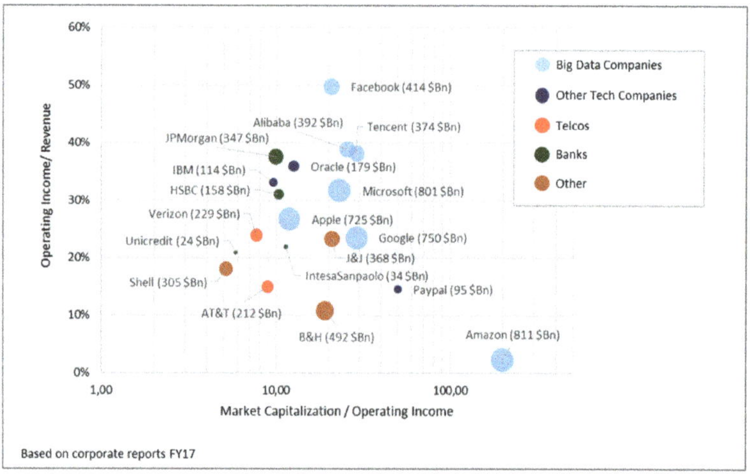

Source: Authors' elaboration from corporate reports FY2017.

5 By way of comparison, the Italian panel Auditel is made up of 16,100 families, around 41,000 individuals, as against Facebook's 30 million Italian users.

6 A visibility that resembles Walter Benjamin's thoughts in *The Work of Art in the Age of Mechanical Reproduction* (1935) about readers becoming authors, including solely 'letters to the editor'. Leaving to one side the relatively small number of 'influencers' who have built personal businesses on the visibility acquired, effectively making themselves testimonials for commercial brands to a greater or lesser extent. We have also left out the use of social media to disseminate political messages, the subject of intense debate today around the responsibility of platform providers for this, especially in the event of powerfully discriminatory or terrorist contents. See, for example, Singer and Brooking (2018).

The pervasive nature of Big Tech in the digital world and its ability to track online behaviours has been illustrated by a report produced by Oxford University's computer science department (Binns 2018). The British researchers have analysed the phenomenon of 'third-party tracking', namely the potential for service supplier websites and apps ('first party') to include a code segment traceable to a 'third party' advertising supplier who installs a cookie in the user's browser which enables it to track user-surfing on all sites and apps using the same code. From a sample of 5,000 websites and 5,000 apps the following situation has been detected.[7]

Table 3: Presence on apps.

		Presence on Apps (%)				
		< 10	< 25	< 50	< 75	> 75
Web presence (%)	> 75					
	< 75					Google
	< 50				Facebook	
	< 25	Amazon Camscore Yieldex Adobe Oracle			Twitter	
	< 10			Yahoo Microsoft PayPal		

The activism of Facebook (38 per cent of websites and 64 per cent of apps) and Google (74 per cent of websites and 94 per cent of apps – in this case fostered by the dissemination of the Android operating system) is confirmed.

The pervasiveness of Big Tech will be further strengthened with the growing diffusion of voice-controlled domestic interactive devices (for example, Amazon Echo and Google Home Assistant) and of the most advanced 'smart home' solutions. Purely by way of example: in January 2018 Google patented the use of always-on optical sensors able to track changes in colours in skin to detect possible cardiovascular alterations; in October 2018 Amazon was granted a patent to detect 'abnormal' voice conditions (from simple cough and sore throat up to identifying emotional states).

7 Note that the main 'trackers', in addition to Big Tech and firms such as Yieldex and CamScore, also include firms such as Adobe and Oracle.

The potential applications are countless, but so are the implications from the data protection point of view.

2. GDPR as an awareness-raising tool

In a speech at the opening session of the fortieth privacy guarantee conference in Brussels (Buttarelli 2018) and also in some of his interviews (Guasco 2018, Del Re 2018), European Data Protection Supervisor Giovanni Buttarelli – one of those who inspired the GDPR – highlighted that personal data processing abuses are not only a deplorable business practice[8] but they could also also constitute a risk for democracy.[9] In fact, he speaks specifically of an ethical approach to the issue when he argues that 'today everything that is technically sustainable and legally doable is morally debatable'. In speculation about an 'extreme' scenario, we must also consider that since citizens are getting more and more used to referring to a single platform for their interaction with the digital world, that platform has the potential opportunity to drive their feelings as electors by controlling or simply influencing the access to the information upon which the public opinion is formed. And we must not forget as well that the principles inspiring the governance rules of the global platforms, even in a context of full formal compliance to laws and regulations,[10] could be conceived in countries with a substantially different cultural background and sensibility (regarding, for example, customer protection) compared to European ones.

It is on these bases that the GDPR was conceived, underlining certain overall elements: (1) the definition of 'personal data': any information relating to an identified or identifiable individual, a definition which considerably extends the

8 The widely reported Cambridge Analytica case, that led to a formal judicial case by the District of Columbia against Facebook and the more recent issue raised by the *New York Times* regarding a supposed 'trust' among the Big Techs to share users' data (see for instance Sarcina 2018) are considerably raising the attention level and the burden of the consequences. Mark Zuckerberg himself in a message posted at the end of 2018 stated that it will take years to solve all the problems related to security, privacy and interference, also adding a future commitment to a stronger proactive approach against misuses. See Frier (2018).

9 'Big Data algorithms might create digital dictatorships in which all power is concentrated in the hands of a tiny elite while most people suffer not from exploitation, but from something far worse–irrelevance.' Harari (2018: xvi). Also to be carefully considered is the power that can be gained by a government over its citizens, as in the Chinese 'social credit' system. See Ma (2018).

10 And a 'don't be evil' good intention in corporate motto.

regulations application perimeter; (2) the inalienable nature of 'data ownership' which remains the reference individual's with related rights to cancel, rectify and transfer; (3) the constancy of data responsibility duties regarding the methods and purposes for which the data are processed: the fact that a service is free in no way lessens these duties.

It follows that individuals know that neither their 'ownership' of their personal data nor their responsibility for the production of the data can be limited, in any circumstances. They thus have the right to be informed (which can also be understood as their duty to find out) about the purposes for which data are collected and processed. Moreover, the firms which collect and use data (the data controllers, in GDPR terminology) must be aware of their responsibilities to individuals in terms of transparency and coherence and act consequently.

This leads to an overall change of perspective: from an approach which links the concept of privacy to that of 'protection' (understood as constraints on access and juxtaposed to the concept of 'sharing'[11]), to an idea of privacy as 'safeguards', namely defence against misuse and damage. This translates into a strong stance relating to: limitations on processing which must be authorized in advance and limited to the purposes it was authorized for; data collection limitations which must be relevant to authorized purposes and limited to what is necessary for these; data protection against illegal use.

Informed individuals can thus choose, in accordance with the 'spirit of the times', which data to share and for which purposes. This can thus be regarded as an evolution from the past's 'unconscious sharing' to 'conscious sharing', which is the objective. It is comparable with the difference between a national park and a forest managed with sustainability criteria defined by Programme for the Endorsement of Forest Certification (PEFC) in the field of forest resource exploitation.

Does the GDPR jeopardize the Big Tech business model? Probably not, or at least not to a determinant extent. In fact, it might be said, as many analysts and commentators have noted, that the correct implementation of the safeguard measures set out involves an operational and technological effort the cost of which can be borne more easily by large firms with their solid profits and investment capacities than by small providers or, to an even greater extent, by start-ups. The dominance of Big Tech would, thus, be paradoxically strengthened.[12]

---

11 In a 2010 interview, Mark Zuckerberg stated: 'My concept of privacy is not the same as my father's and it differs from that of a boy of fourteen [...]. For my parents, privacy was a value, for my peers sharing is a value.' See Stahl (2018).

12 Moreover, it is not the task of the privacy guarantor to enter into the merits of dominant markets, which is the jurisdiction of antitrust bodies. On this subject it should

Apple CEO Tim Cook's statements to the Brussel's conference in which he expressed his strong appreciation of GDPR and hoped that the model would be adopted by the USA and the rest of the world are interesting in this regard.[13] Erin Egan, Facebook's privacy spokesperson, has expressed similar views. Those directly affected, probably more in a defensive logic than out of any sincere belief, would seem to support the GDPR, even in opposition to the US government whose commerce secretary Wilbur Ross, whilst recognising the importance of safeguarding personal data, expressed strong concerns on the subject of the potentially negative effects of European regulation on international trade (Ross 2018).

3. Digital ID and data sovereignty as possible rebalancing factors

Assuming that the GDPR does not significantly influence the Big Tech business model, the question is whether it can, in some way, diminish the 'digital dividend' as intended and cited repeatedly by Buttarelli (D'Alessandro 2018), namely the lack of a citizen share (as individuals and communities) in the profits Big Tech earns by processing the data of these same citizens.

Returning to a by now commonly used analogy according to which 'data is the new oil', the firms active in the oil sector 'redistribute' their profits in two ways (in addition to shareholder dividends): indirectly by taxes[14] and directly by paying

---

be highlighted that the online advertising market generated 203 billion dollars in 2017 with Google's share being 47 per cent and Facebook's 19 per cent. (Bernard 2018). The US Federal Trade Commission launched a series of hearings on the subject of competition and consumer protection in the big data context. Of note in Europe are the fines incurred by Google in June 2018 for abuses of their dominant position on the Android operating system; initiatives by EU Commissar Margrethe Vestager who launched an enquiry into Amazon and the action of German antitrust supervisor Andreas Mundt who formally accused Facebook of abusing its dominant position.

13 Tim Cook has adopted a powerfully critical stance relating to Big Tech and in favour of greater privacy on other occasions too. See, for example, his speech at EPIC 2015 Champions of Freedom, Washington, in June 2015. 'We believe that people have a fundamental right to privacy. The American people demand it, the constitution demands it, morality demands it.' (Panzarino 2015) For the sake of completeness, it is important to specify that Apple highlights the 'inviolability' of its products as a distinctive factor, even opposing the specific requests of the FBI for assistance with accessing blocked devices (Holpuch 2016).

14 The issue of taxing global platform operators has been the subject of wide-ranging debate by the competent authorities and is outside the scope of this study.

royalties to countries in which oil has been found.[15] If Facebook paid royalties as a percentage of revenues comparable with those of the oil firms, the billions of users active on a monthly basis would be entitled to just over one dollar each. This is probably not the right approach.[16]

Building an alternative hypothesis involves starting from the most important of the characteristics differentiating digital data from physical products of any kind: the potential for reproducing them indefinitely without any loss in their characteristics (pre-Internet era) which has evolved into the potential for simultaneous and substantially unlimited use (social era).

The objective to move towards, made possible by combining the data transfer rights introduced in the GDPR[17] with the evolution of the technologies, is to enable individuals to exercise 'sovereignty' over their data.

The use of the term 'sovereignty' expresses not only a form of technical and practical control over the access to data, but also that the right to exercise comes from a collectively acknowledged source of legitimacy.

The starting point is the individual's identity management in the digital space. The attributes of personal data include the potential for them to be associated with 'identified and identifiable' individuals. It is in the interests of individuals and institutions[18] that identification is certain, linking data to a single digital ID across the whole digital ecosystem. In the European Union the eIDAS Regulation, which came into force in September 2018, aims at the creation of a digital identity ecosystem. Italy was, on this occasion, a first mover with the SPID – Sistema Pubblico di Identità Digitale (Public Digital Identity System) – which has not, however, reached a significant critical mass as yet.

15 To give a general idea, in 2017 Eni paid 674 million euro in royalties, around 3 per cent of its Exploration and Production division's profits (source: Eni 2018). Only by coincidence, the Italian 2019 budget law introduces a 3 per cent tax on revenues from digital services to be applied to companies with more than 750 million euro turnover of which at least 5.5 million generated in Italy from digital services.

16 Some startups (like CitizenMe, Datacoup, Weople) propose a model where they act as intermediaries between consumers and Big Tech firms, guaranteeing to the former an economic return. Datacoup, for example, estimates an average value of $1.5.

17 In Article 20 the GDPR specifies that individuals have the right to require data controllers to make their personal data available and, if technically feasible, transfer it to an alternative data controller.

18 Note that in Italy, for example, offensive comments on social media or other IT systems can be considered printed libel (see Corte di Cassazione sentence 24431/2015 among others) and thus a certain form of author identification may be necessary for these ends too.

The ID2020 Alliance initiative is worthy of mention[19] as it has set itself the objective of supplying a billion people in developing areas with a form of legal identity which would bring them out of a forced state of 'invisibility' which denies them access to fundamental rights. ID2020 Alliance's activities have developed in two directions: (1) technology – development of standards and specifications which simplify the development of interoperable solutions; and (2) delivery – development of partnerships with public and private organizations with broad delivery networks.

ID2020 Alliance plans to select and fund pilot projects to assess costs, requisites, opportunities and risks associated with the different approaches.

The self-sovereign identity concept is built on digital ID and consists of the potential for individuals to create a repository of all the information related to them protected by cryptographic algorithms and certified, all from competent third-party bodies (such as town councils for personal data, school boards for qualifications, and so on) in such a way as to make them non-modifiable.[20] Therefore, a citizen's identity is independent from any single third party (that is, a service provider) and can be unequivocally associated to every data element related to the citizen. The use of blockchain/DLT[21] technologies can facilitate the creation of the model thanks to the potential for easily guaranteeing data certainty and inalterability (so-called 'notarization' features).

In a forward-looking perspective this could make possible the logical separation between data and applications theorized by Tim Berners-Lee as long ago as 2009 and taken up by Francesco Bernabè in 2012 with the concept of personal data space (PDS) (see Berners Lee 2009, Bernabè 2012).

Essentially each network-connected individual can make use of a personal archive space (the PDS) in which all their personal data can be stored, wherever and whenever they were generated, and linked to their digital ID. Individuals can thus create a 'digital trace' and subsequently give access to this information, in accordance with defined contractual conditions, to third parties who accord

---

19 The Alliance's founders include: Microsoft, Accenture, GAVI, The Rockefeller Foundation.

20 For a more complete consideration of the subject see Der et al. (2017).

21 DLT – distributed ledger technologies – are defined as the processes and related technologies that enable nodes in a network to securely propose, validate and record state changes (or updates) to a synchronized ledger that is distributed across a network's nodes according to a pre-defined consensus mechanism. Blockchain is a declination of the DLT model where each transaction is linked, by means of cryptographic algorithms, to previous transactions.

them the value generated by it in monetary or service terms. These contractual conditions would regulate all access authorizations and data use including sharing levels (of data), time frames (for how long data is accessible) and the purposes for which they are to be used.

Various initiatives, at the moment still in a research/experimentation stage, are pursuing the implementation of this vision. Among them: the Solid project, being developed by MIT under Tim Berners-Lee's guidance; and European PoSeID-on (Protection and Control of Secured Information by Means of a Privacy Enhanced Dashboard) and Papaya (PlAtform for PrivAcY preserving data Analytics) projects co-funded by the European Commission within the framework of the Horizon 2020 programme.

Solid is an open source project (with a commercial structure thanks to startup Inrupt launched in 2018) which aims to create: a collection of standards and data format/dictionaries which provide the same services supplied by the centralized social media, such as identity, authentication, login, authorization lists, contacts management, messaging, feed subscription, and so on; specifications and project notes which describe a REST API[22] to extend existing standards and guide developers in application building; servers which implement Solid specifications; a test-suite to test and validate Solid implementations; an ecosystem of social applications, identity providers and bookstores operating on the Solid platform; and a community which supplies documentation, discussions, tutorials and presentations.

The PoSeID-on project's goal is to create a platform defined as a 'privacy-enhanced dashboard' which gives individuals a tool for easy, concise, transparent and user-friendly access and a tracking tool for all their personal data processed by public and private organizations. They will thus be able to take decisions relating to whom they allow to process their data, issuing or revoking authorizations and being warned in the event of abuses. The deliverables expected by the PoSeID-on project can be summarized as: (1) privacy-enhanced dashboard as an integrated prototype in an ICT architecture usable by organizations wanting to supplement their procedures with a tool designed with GDPR in mind; (2) open source or API components which can potentially be integrated into any private or public ICT architecture; (3) a cloud-based privacy-enhanced dashboard as a service (PEDaaS) solution in favour of organizations which have decided not to, or are not able to, adopt in-house solutions.

---

22 A REST API s an application program interface that uses HTTP requests to manage data.

And all this by promoting high-potential emerging technologies such as DLT/ blockchains and smart contracts[23].

On its side, Papaya's objective is to design and develop data analytics modules which accord with GDPR requirements. Papaya development follows four guidelines: (1) privacy-by-design with the introduction of specific privacy-enhancing technologies; (2) use of different modules in inter-operable mode on a single platform; in addition to privacy safeguard modules the platform will supply specific users (such as developers) the following cryptographic primitives (for example, secure multi-party computation) which can be exploited by future data analytics modules; (3) usability and transparency (including control measures); and (4) auditability, guaranteeing interested parties the ability to check how the Papaya platform works in relation to the data supplied.

Since we have introduced DLT and smart contracts, it might be interesting to outline a long-term scenario.

It is theoretically conceivable to have a model where data are encrypted and stored in a DLT structure, ensuring protection against misuse with the additional benefit of a distributed infrastructure with a high level of resilience. The citizen could set out in a smart contract the data access rules: who can access them, for which purposes, on which conditions. A third party could submit a request and access is allowed only once all the conditions have been fulfilled.

4. Target model, expected benefits and open questions

In conclusion, combining technological solutions and the regulatory framework can lead to the creation of a framework like that shown in Figure 23.

23 A 'smart contract' is a computer code that automatically, and in most cases in an irrevocable manner, executes a set of operations. The concept is not strictly related to legal contracts, but a smart contract can be implemented to securely enforce the execution of one or more contractual obligations.

Figure 23: Model on personal identity regulation.

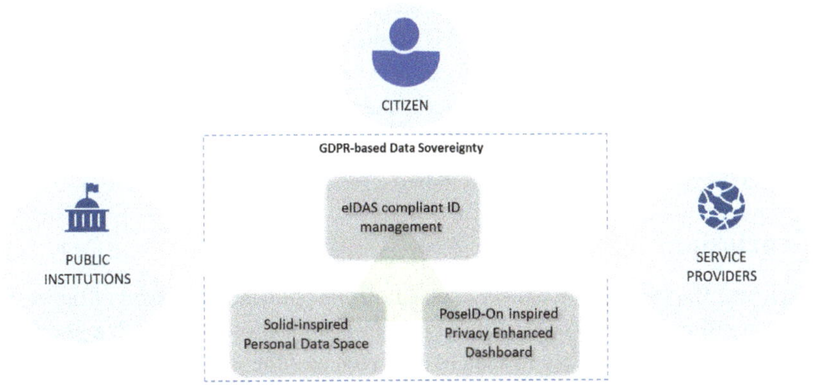

Source: Authors' elaboration.

What might the positive effects of introducing such a model be?

Individuals will be able to reaffirm their ownership of and maintain control over their personal data and decide if, how and with whom to share their personal data and in exchange for which specific benefits.

Public institutions and research bodies could take advantage of this information, supplemented by the data made available in an open data/open government context for their own institutional purposes, guaranteeing full individual rights safeguards.

Access to the extremely high volume of information made up of aggregate PDS would also enable new suppliers and startups to develop original service models, overcoming the 'entrance barriers' constituted by the time frames required to construct a sufficiently large user base. Specifically, the chance to work with large data volumes is fundamental to artificial intelligence developments, the 'next big thing'.

Service suppliers (Big Tech itself) could access a set of information even larger than that which they currently manage[24] but according to specific conditions negotiated with individuals.

The implementation of a PDS model poses a question: who would be responsible for supplying this service? As it is unlikely that individual citizen-users of the network are able to autonomously implement and manage data space, it is theoretically possible that this service can be supplied by a third party, obviously in full conformity with the GDPR. The options are twofold: PDS is considered a public service

24 It should not be ignored that since PSD2 came into force, individuals have been able to allow third parties access to their bank accounts for informative purposes.

and must thus be supplied by a state body. Pushing the matter to its extremes and considering personal data as a personal attribute like any other, PDS can be seen as a sort of extension of national data; PDS is not a public service (although it can be considered useful to the public) and can thus be supplied by private bodies only, in the context of a specific legal framework, like any other service.

If the latter option comes to the fore, the benefits of introducing the PDS would be supplemented by the creation of a new PDS market service.

Conclusions

Each year the prestigious weekly magazine *Time* publishes a 'person of the year' photo on the cover of its December issue. In 2006 it chose to publish a photo of a PC with a mirror surface instead of its screen and the word 'You',[25] as a tribute to all the people who had anonymously contributed to the extraordinary success of the social networks and 'user generated contents' in general. As is traditional, a year later an article at the back of the journal critically analysed the previous year's cover and, in 2007, 'You' was replaced by 'Them' to take stock of the fact that control of the digital world was solidly in the hands of Big Tech.[26]

Figure 24: The future of digital identities.

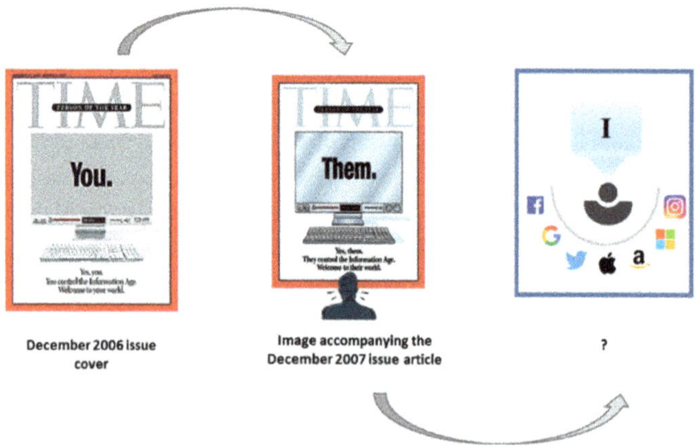

25 'And for seizing the reins of the global media, for founding and framing the new digital democracy, for working for nothing and beating the pros at their own game, TIME's Person of the Year for 2006 is you.' See Grossman (2006).

26 'It's still your world, after all. They just pretend to run it.' See Poniewozik (2007).

More than ten years later, the new consciousness level about the value of personal data could perhaps bring people back to the digital centre-stage in an appropriately ethical and respectful framework.

References

Alexandre, Laurent (2017), *La guerre des intelligences. Comment l'intelligence artificielle va révolutionner l'éducation*, Paris, JC Lattès.

Benjamin, Walter (2008), *The Work of Art in the Age of Mechanical Reproduction*, London, Penguin.

Bernabè, Francesco (2012), *Libertà vigilata. Privacy, sicurezza e mercato nella rete*, Roma/Bari, Laterza.

Bernard, Zoë (2018), "Facebook Accounts for 20% of the Global Online Ad Market", in *Business Insider*, 28 March.

Berners-Lee, Tim (2009), 'Socially Aware Cloud Storage', in *w3*, 17 August, https://www.w3.org/DesignIssues/CloudStorage.html.

Binns, Reuben et al. (2018), "Measuring Third-Party Tracker Power across Web and Mobile", in *ACM Transactions on Internet Technology (TOIT)*, Vol. 18, No. 4 (November), Art. 52.

Buttarelli, Giovanni (2018), '40th ICDPPC: Opening Speech by Giovanni Buttarelli. Choose Humanity: Putting Dignity Back into Digital', in *European Data Protection Law Review*, Vol. 4, no. 4, p. vii-x, https://edpl.lexxion.eu/article/EDPL/2018/4/25.

D'Alessandro, Jaime (2018), 'La direttiva europea sulla privacy sta diventando uno standard mondiale', in *Repubblica Affari e Finanza*, 15 October, p. 47.

Del Re, Giovanni Maria (2018), 'Il Garante Ue della privacy. "Stop al monopolio dei dati. In gioco c'è la democrazia"', in *Avvenire*, 25 October, https://www.avvenire.it/attualita/pagine/stop-al-monopolio-dei-dati-in-gioco-c-la-democrazia.

Der, Uwe, Stefan Jähnichen and Jan Sürmeli (2017), 'Self-sovereign Identity – Opportunities and Challenges for the Digital Revolution', in *arXiv Preprints*, 5 December, https://arxiv.org/abs/1712.01767.

Eni (2018), *Annual Report on Form 20-F 2017*, https://www.eni.com/docs/en_IT/enicom/publications-archive/publications/reports/rapporti-2017/Annual-Report-On-Form-20-F-2017.pdf.

Frier, Sarah (2018), 'Facebook CEO Zuckerberg Says Problems Will Take Years to Fix', in *Bloomberg*, 28 December, https://www.bloomberg.com/news/articles/2018-12-28/facebook-ceo-zuckerberg-says-problems-will-take-years-to-fix.

Grossman, Lev (2006), 'You – Yes, You – Are TIME's Person of the Year', in *Time*, 25 December, http://content.time.com/time/magazine/article/0,9171,1570810,00.html.

Guasco, Claudia (2018), 'Buttarelli: "Ma i dati vanno condivisi, gli utenti non sono dei polli digitali"', in *Il Messaggero*, 16 October, p. 19.

Harari, Yuval Noah (2018), *21 lessons for the 21st Century*, New York, Penguin Random.

Holpuch, Amanda (2016), 'Tim Cook Says Apple's Refusal to Unlock iPhone for FBI is a "Civil Liberties" Issue', in *The Guardian*, 22 February, https://gu.com/p/4hxx4.

Ma, Alexandra (2018), 'China Has Started Ranking Citizens with a Creepy "Social Credit" System…', in *Business Insider*, 29 October, https://www.businessinsider.com/china-social-credit-system-punishments-and-rewards-explained-2018-4.

Panzarino, Matthew (2015), 'Apple's Tim Cook Delivers Blistering Speech on Encryption, Privacy', in *TechCrunch*, 2 June, https://techcrunch.com/?p=1166324.

Poniewozik, James (2007), 'The Year of Them', in *Time*, 19 December, http://content.time.com/time/specials/2007/personoftheyear/article/0,28804,1690753_1695417_1695397,00.html.

Regulation (EU) 2016/679 of 27 April 2016 on the Protection of Natural Persons with Regard to the Processing of Personal Data and on the Free Movement of Such Data, and repealing Directive 95/46/EC (General Data Protection Regulation), http://data.europa.eu/eli/reg/2016/679/oj.

Ross, Wilbur (2018), 'EU Data Privacy Laws Are Likely to Create Barriers to Trade', in *Financial Times*, 30 May, https://www.ft.com/content/9d261f44-6255-11e8-bdd1-cc0534df682c.

Sarcina, Giuseppe (2018), 'Facebook alla sbarra negli Usa: "cartello" con Netflix e altri big', in *Corriere della Sera*, 20 December, https://www.corriere.it/tecnologia/18_dicembre_20/facebook-sbarra-usa-cartello-netflix-altri-big-db020074-03e2-11e9-94ba-cb54e059ac5f.shtml.

Singer, P.W. and Emerson T. Brooking (2018), *LikeWar. The Weaponization of Social Media*, Boston/New York, Houghton Mifflin Harcourt.

Stahl, Lesley (2010), 'Mark Zuckerberg and Facebook: What's Next?', in *CBS News*, 1 December, https://www.cbsnews.com/news/mark-zuckerberg-and-facebook-whats-next.

Nicola Bilotta and Simone Romano

Conclusion

The technological revolution that has been reshaping our societies is overhauling the way business is made or even conceived. Industrial structures and firm organizations have been deeply affected by these game-changing transformations. The banking industry is one of the sectors most affected by fast-paced changes that are reducing entry barriers and increasing disintermediation processes, resulting in a fiercer competition landscape.

Large technological and non-financial companies (Techfins) are currently entering key segments of the banking supply chain, taking advantage of their privileged relationship with consumers previously developed in their commercial and industrial activity and exploiting advanced technical solutions.

Techfins' intention to provide banking services responds to two main goals: (i) generating valuable data on the profile of individuals, improving the quality of their personal information, and (ii) becoming more relevant in consumers' life. Their marketing products and services gain from also offering banking services, by continuously engaging customers and meeting their needs inside their ecosystem. This phenomenon is confirmed by the two case studies discussed in this book – Alibaba in China and Rakuten in Japan, which have developed banking services and products.

The analysis and evidence presented in this book have shown that even if tech giants can enjoy many comparative advantages when entering the banking sector, so far they do not seem willing to become fully licensed banks. This can be explained in light of the high compliance costs and the tight regulation of the banking industry. Nonetheless, the key transformations brought about by PSD2 – the new European regulatory framework on payments – in its attempt to foster competitiveness and innovations are likely to incentivize tech giants' penetration in the payment and money-management segments. The PSD2 allows consumers to manage their accounts also through third-party applications and it enables data portability, giving the opportunity to consumers to share their banking information with third-party providers. Incumbents have raised concerns about tech giants enjoying an asymmetric regulatory framework because the PSD2 does not provide reciprocal access to data: tech giants can gain access to a client's banking information once they acquire an e-money and payment licence, but banks do not have any means to access the huge amount of data held by tech giants.

Beyond regulatory requirements, Techfins might not be interested in becoming strict competitors of incumbents due to their deep commercial relationships with them. Banks have become excellent customers of technology-driven services provided by tech giants, such as cloud-based infrastructures, AI and blockchain solutions, aimed at reducing their operating costs. These mutually beneficial ventures provide great business opportunities to both sides: tech giants expand their offer to their consumers, strengthening their brands and accessing further data, whereas banks can access the large base of tech giants' clients. Albeit this can on the surface appear to be a win–win scenario, it actually fosters imbalances between incumbents and tech giants, with the former increasing their dependence on the latter, which – in turn – are increasing their bargaining power over the former. In this way big tech companies can extend their range of banking services without exposing their balance sheets to risks and compliance costs, also eroding margins in segments where banks used to have a monopoly.

The partnership between big banks and tech giants may also result in the concentration of market power among a small number of corporate giants, reducing market competitiveness. Nonetheless, from a strict antitrust perspective, as long as tech giants comply with national and international regulations, their progressive entrance into the banking services' business could reduce transaction costs and generate huge benefits for consumers, resulting in a better functioning of the market.

Overall, considering the pivotal role of the banking industry for the functioning of the global economy, the entrance of tech giants into the financial sector needs to be carefully scrutinized and monitored from a policy perspective. Digitalization can naturally lead to 'a-winner-takes-most-(if not all)-game' scenario due to network effects. Given their key role in the network economy, tech giants can gain immense bargaining power which could give them a role in our societies and economies that no private institution has ever had.

This huge power, together with the intangible nature of their core business, has been often used by tech giants to avoid taxes, resulting in base erosion and profit-shifting practices. The sizeable liquidity coming from these tax avoidance practices can reinforce their dominant position: it can be invested in R&D, further strengthening their technological leadership, or it can be invested in the global financial markets, resulting in a portfolio with a market value comparable to that of the main investment banks. It remains to be seen whether the current efforts of fiscal authorities – aimed at better coordinating their policies and possibly achieving a harmonized taxation framework – will be able to prevent a race to the bottom and to better distribute the gains from technological progress.

These developments inevitably raise political concerns. Tech giants have grounded their business models on mining, aggregating and analysing personal data for commercial purposes. This accumulation of individual data concentrated in a few platforms is going to be reinforced if tech giants access banking data as well, potentially incentivizing moral hazard to unauthorized commercial uses of banking personal information. These mechanisms of cross-sources data aggregation may also constitute a challenge to democratic norms unless current regulations succeed in preventing mismanagement of personal data.

However, the offering of financial services by tech companies may spur the adoption of a single, secure and safe digital identity, opening new business opportunities for established banks. Due to their expertise in managing physical and digital identities, banks could become hubs of a multi-purpose digital identity – a sort of 'digital passport' – which could be used by customers to access different services in their online ecosystem, reducing inefficiency and time-consumption, and, as a consequence, reinforcing banks' centrality in consumers' lives.

The future of banking will depend on how incumbents embrace the challenges of digital and technology transformations, converting threats into opportunities. However, tech giants' expansion in banking has implications that go well beyond the boundaries of the industry and should be carefully considered. The challenge is not to halt this multifaceted technological revolution but to steer it towards a sustainable and inclusive improvement of our society and economy.

GLOBAL POLITICS AND SECURITY

Series Editor:
Prof. Lorenzo Kamel,
University of Turin's History Department,
and Istituto Affari Internazionali (IAI)

"Global Politics and Security" publishes high-quality books authored by leading academics, think-tankers and policymakers on topical questions in international relations and contemporary history, ranging from diplomacy and security, to development, economy, migration, energy and climate. The series publishes works produced by the Istituto Affari Internazionali (IAI), Italy's leading foreign policy think-tank, as well as by authors affiliated to other international think tanks or universities. The aim is to promote deeper knowledge of emerging issues and trends through constant exchange between the worlds of academia and practice. Publications include original monographs and edited volumes which combine a grasp of the past, an understanding of present dynamics, and a vision about potential futures.

Vol. 1 Lorenzo Colantoni, Giuseppe Montesano, Nicolò Sartori (eds): Empowering Africa. Access to power in the African continent.

Vol. 2 Aybars Görgülü, Gulsah Dark Kahyaoğlu (eds): The Remaking of the Euro-Mediterranean Vision. Challenging Eurocentrism with Local Perceptions in the Middle East and North Africa.

Vol. 3 Leila Simona Talani, Matilde Rosina (eds): Tidal Waves? The Political Economy of Populism and Migration in Europe.

Vol. 4 Nicola Bilotta, Simone Romano (eds): The Rise of Tech Giants. A Game Changer in Global Finance and Politics.

Vol. 5 Lorenzo Kamel (ed.): The Middle East: Thinking About and Beyond Security and Stability.

www.ingramcontent.com/pod-product-compliance
Ingram Content Group UK Ltd.
Pitfield, Milton Keynes, MK11 3LW, UK
UKHW021847100926
8556IPUK00020B/1099

9 783034 338486